MINI Map+Guide
PRAGUE

CONTENTS

EXPERIENCE

NEED TO KNOW

Left: Magnificent Charles Bridge at sunset
Right: Church of Our Lady Before Týn

Penguin
Random
House

Main Contributors Marc Di Duca, Vladimir Soukup

Design Nidhi Mehra, Priyanka Thakur

Editorial Rachel Fox, Shikha Kulkarni,
Beverly Smart, Manjari Thakur

Indexer Kanika Praharaj

Picture Research Sumita Khatwani, Ellen Root

Cartography Suresh Kumar, Casper Morris

Jacket Designers Maxine Pedliham, Amy Cox

DTP Narender Kumar, Jason Little, Tanveer Zaidi

Delhi Team Head Malavika Talukder

Art Director Maxine Pedliham

Publishing Director Georgina Dee

Conceived by Priyanka Thakur
and Shikha Kulkarni

Printed and bound in China

Content previously published in DK Eyewitness
Prague (2019). This abridged edition first
published in 2020
Published in Great Britain by
Dorling Kindersley Limited
80 Strand, London WC2R 0RL

Published in the United States by DK Publishing,
1450 Broadway, Suite 801, New York, NY 10018

19 20 21 22 10 9 8 7 6 5 4 3 2 1

A CIP catalogue record is available
from the British Library.

A catalogue record for this book is available
from the Library of Congress.
ISBN 978-0-2413-9776-3

**The information in this DK Eyewitness
Travel Guide is checked regularly.**
Every effort has been made to ensure this book
is up-to-date at the time of going to press.
However, details such as addresses, opening
hours, prices and travel information, are liable to
change. The publishers cannot accept
responsibility for any consequences arising
from the use of this book, nor for any
material on third-party websites. If you
have any comments, please write to: DK
Eyewitness Travel Guides, Dorling Kindersley,
80 Strand, London WC2R 0RL, UK, or email:
travelguides@dk.com.

KEY TO MAIN ICONS

📍	Map	🚌	Bus
🏠	Address/Location	ℹ️	Visitor information
📞	Telephone	🕐	Open
🚆	Train	🔒	Closed
Ⓜ	Metro	🌐	Website
🚋	Tram		

MIX
Paper from
responsible sources
FSC™ C018179

WELCOME TO
PRAGUE

Art Nouveau masterpieces jostling with
Communist-era bombast, a rich classical music
heritage echoing through medieval streets and
the planet's best beer enjoyed on Baroque squares –
Prague is a cultural mosaic. Whatever your ideal
break to Prague includes, this DK Eyewitness Mini
Map and Guide is the perfect travel companion.

This city has firmly established itself as one of Europe's most engaging – all who visit are bewitched by the spires and the cobbles, the shadows and the tiny lanes. The medieval splendour of the Old Town Square, where the Old Town Hall's Astronomical Clock still chimes the hour, and Gothic Charles Bridge continue to dazzle. Trams trundle past the world's biggest castle complex, dominated by St Vitus's Cathedral, the nation's religious epicentre. Architectural treasures like the Art Nouveau phenomenon that is the Municipal House and the Baroque St Nicholas Cathedral, plus the mysterious atmosphere of the sights belonging to the Jewish Museum, testify to this city's rich history. And in between, don't forget to take time out to enjoy Prague's unsurpassed beer in one of its characterful pubs and beer halls.

Prague is the capital of the Czech Republic, a wonderful destination in its own right. The country has more castles than any other – top of the list are the three Ks, Karlštejn, Konopiště and Křivoklát – all easy day trips. For a bit of R&R, head west to the spa towns of Karlovy Vary and Mariánské Lázně, both of which offer world-class facilities and countless possibilities for hiking in Bohemia's endless forests.

From Vyšehrad to Prague Castle, we break Prague down into easily navigable chapters, highlighting each area's unmissable sights and unexpected delights. Add insider tips, a comprehensive fold-out map and a need-to-know section full of expert advice for before and during your trip, and you've got an indispensable guidebook. Enjoy the book, and enjoy Prague.

↓ The Vltava flowing through Prague.

STARÉ MĚSTO

Hemmed in by the River Vltava on two sides, Prague's Old Town is what the crowds of tourists who flock to the Czech capital come to see. Prague's medieval epicentre is the Old Town Square from which crooked streets shoot off in every direction. One of these, Karlova, leads to Charles Bridge and is the main tourist route through the city. The Old Town is also where most people want to stay, the quarter possessing many characterful but pricey hotels. Eating options are good here, but watch out for overpriced touristy spots, especially around the Old Town Square.

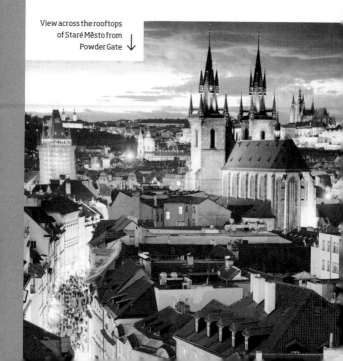

View across the rooftops of Staré Město from Powder Gate ↓

OLD TOWN SQUARE
STAROMĚSTSKÉ NÁMĚSTÍ

📍H4 🏛Staré Město

As the heart and soul of the city, no visitor should, or is likely to, miss the Old Town Square. Free of traffic and ringed with historic buildings, it ranks among the finest public spaces in any city. The square is always buzzing; in winter and summer, it's a wonderful place to enjoy a coffee or a mug of beer and watch the world go by. Although the area draws visitors in droves, its unique atmosphere has prevailed.

23,000

sq metres (247,570 sq ft) of new paving was laid in the square during reconstruction work in 1987.

There was a marketplace here in the 11th century, but it was not until 1338, when John of Luxembourg gave Prague's burghers permission to form a town council, that the Old Town Hall was built and the square came into its own. Over the centuries, this now peaceful square has witnessed hundreds of executions, political capitulations and riots. Today, it has a lively atmosphere, with café tables set out on the cobbles in front of painted façades, hawkers selling their wares and horse-drawn carriages waiting to ferry tourists around.

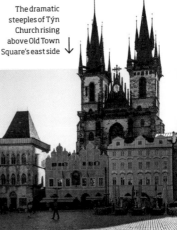

The dramatic steeples of Týn Church rising above Old Town Square's east side ↓

MARIAN COLUMN

From 1650 to 1918, the Baroque Marian Column, topped with a statue of the Virgin Mary, stood in the square and each day at noon its shadow marked the Prague Meridian. On Czechoslovakia's declaration of independence in 1918, the column was torn down by jubilant mobs. Today, a golden metal line in the paving of Old Town Square indicates where the column's shadow was cast; look out for this near the Jan Hus Monument. The remains of the Marian Column are displayed in the Lapidarium in Prague's Exhibition Ground.

EAST AND NORTH SIDES

Some of Prague's colourful history is preserved around the Old Town Square in the form of its buildings. The north side, dominated by the St Nicholas Cathedral, includes the Pauline Monastery, which is the only surviving piece of original architecture. The imposing Church of Our Lady

Before Týn rises up above the square's east side, where there are two superb examples of the architecture of their times: the house At the Stone Bell, restored to its former appearance as a Gothic town palace, and the Rococo Kinský Palace, with its elaborate stucco decoration.

NORTH SIDE   *Ministerstvo pro místní rozvoj, an Art Noveau building*   *Former Pauline Monastery*

SOUTH SIDE

A colourful array of houses of Romanesque or Gothic origin, with fascinating house signs, graces the south side of the Old Town Square. The block between Celetná Street and Železná Street is especially attractive. The ornate Neo-Renaissance Štorch House, adorned with beautiful paintings, stands out. Also of note is At the Stone Table. Originally a Romanesque house that was rebuilt in Gothic style, it features an elaborate 18th-century Baroque façade.

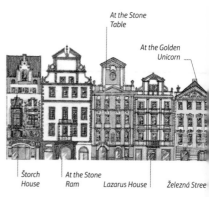

At the Stone Table

At the Golden Unicorn

Štorch House   *At the Stone Ram*   *Lazarus House*   *Železná Street*

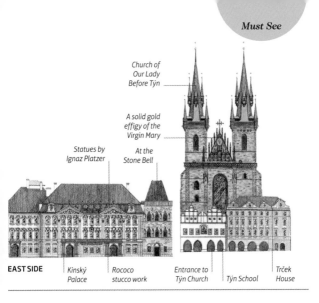

Church of
Our Lady
Before Týn

A solid gold
effigy of the
Virgin Mary

Statues by
Ignaz Platzer

At the
Stone Bell

EAST SIDE | Kinský
Palace | Rococo
stucco work | Entrance to
Týn Church | Týn School | Trček
House

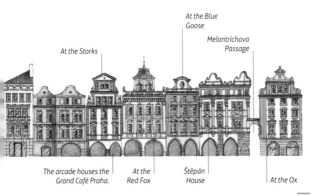

At the Blue
Goose

Melantrichova
Passage

At the Storks

The arcade houses the
Grand Café Praha. | At the
Red Fox | Štěpán
House | At the Ox

OLD TOWN HALL
STAROMĚSTSKÁ RADNICE

🔲H4 🏠Staroměstské náměstí 1 Ⓜ Staroměstská (line A), Můstek (A & B) 🚋17, 18 🕐Tower: 11am-10pm Mon, 9am-10pm Tue-Sun; Halls: 11am-6pm Mon, 9am-6pm Tue-Sun 🌐prague.eu

One of the most striking buildings in Prague is the Old Town Hall, established in 1338 after King John of Luxembourg agreed to set up a town council.

Over the centuries, a number of old houses were knocked together as the Old Town Hall expanded, and it now consists of a row of Gothic and Renaissance buildings, most of which have been carefully restored after heavy damage inflicted by the Nazis in the 1945 Prague Uprising. The tower is 69.5 m (228 ft) high and offers a spectacular view of the city. On the hall's ground floor is an exhibition space used for temporary art shows.

ASTRONOMICAL CLOCK (ORLOJ)

The Town Hall acquired its first clock at the beginning of the 15th century. Though the clock has been repaired many times since, the mechanism was perfected by Jan Táborský between 1552 and 1572. The clock not only tells the time, but also displays the movement of the sun and moon through the signs of the zodiac, and of the planets around the earth. The centrepiece of the show that draws a crowd of spectators every time the clock strikes the hour, between 9am and 11pm, is the procession of the 12 Apostles.

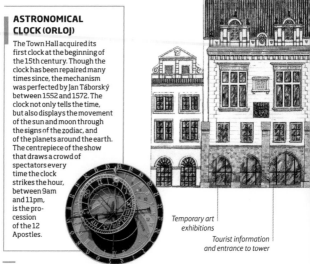

Temporary art exhibitions

Tourist information and entrance to tower

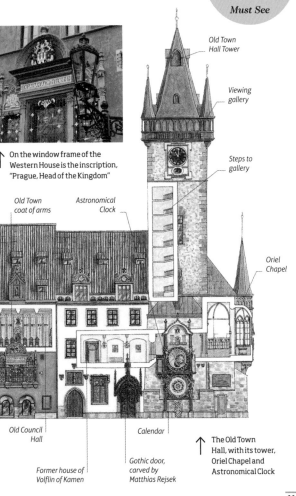

On the window frame of the Western House is the inscription, "Prague, Head of the Kingdom"

Old Town Hall Tower

Viewing gallery

Steps to gallery

Old Town coat of arms

Astronomical Clock

Oriel Chapel

Old Council Hall

Calendar

Former house of Volflin of Kamen

Gothic door, carved by Matthias Rejsek

The Old Town Hall, with its tower, Oriel Chapel and Astronomical Clock

MUNICIPAL HOUSE
OBECNÍ DŮM

📍 K4 🏠 Náměstí Republiky 5 Ⓜ Náměstí Republiky 🚋 6, 8, 15, 26
🕙 10am –8pm daily 🌐 obecnidum.cz

Prague's most prominent Art Nouveau building is well worth visiting to admire the flamboyant and exciting decoration. Discover the stunning interiors on the excellent guided tour, grab a bite to eat in one of the beautiful restaurants or sip a cocktail in Prague's oldest bar.

Municipal House stands on the site of the former Royal Court palace, the residence of the rulers of Bohemia between 1383 and 1485. Abandoned for centuries, what remained was used as a seminary and later as a military college. It was demolished in the early 1900s to be replaced by the current cultural centre in 1911 with its exhibition halls and auditorium, designed by Antonín Balšánek assisted by Osvald Polívka.

The exterior is lavishly decorated with stucco and allegorical statuary. The figures, seen on all sides of the building, are by Czech artists who combined Classical and historic symbols with modern motifs.

Municipal House's stairways
feature fine Art Nouveau details

entire building, the Smetana Hall,
sometimes also used as a ballroom.
The interior is decorated with the works
by the leading artists of the time, most
prominently Alfons Mucha.

Above the main entrance there is a
huge semicircular mosaic entitled
Homage to Prague by Karel Špilar.
Inside, topped by an impressive
glass dome, is Prague's principal
concert venue and the core of the

↑ The Smetana Hall, home to the Prague
Symphony Orchestra, is decorated
with beautiful paintings

ALFONS MUCHA (1860-1939)

National Revival artist Alfons Mucha,
born near Brno, was one of many to lend
his talents to the Municipal House. He
moved to Paris in 1887 and it was here
that he was commissioned to design a
poster for a new play. After an intense
period of poster design, Mucha returned
to Prague in 1910. His greatest work is
the *Slav Epic*, a series of 20 canvases
depicting the history of the Slavs.
Mucha died following interrogation
by the Gestapo in 1939.

← The impressive
Municipal House
building, with its
iconic glass dome

EXPERIENCE MORE

Basilica of St James
Bazilika Sv. Jakuba

Ⓠ J4 **Ⓜ** Malá Štupartská 6 **Ⓒ** 224 828 816 **Ⓜ** Můstek, Náměstí Republiky **Ⓒ** 9:30am-noon & 2-4pm Tue-Sat (to 3:30pm Fri), 2-4pm Sun

This basilica was originally the Gothic presbytery of a Minorite monastery. The order (a branch of the Franciscans) was invited to Prague by King Wenceslas I in 1232. The church was rebuilt in the Baroque style after a fire in 1689, allegedly started by agents of Louis XIV. More than 20 side altars were added, decorated with works by painters such as Jan Jiří Heinsch, Petr Brandl and Václav Vavřinec Reiner.

The tomb of Count Vratislav of Mitrovice, designed by Johann Bernhard Fischer von Erlach and executed by sculptor Ferdinand Brokoff, was completed in 1714 and is the most beautiful Baroque tomb in Bohemia. The count is said to have been accidentally buried alive – his corpse was later found sitting up in the tomb.

Hanging on the right of the entrance is a mummified forearm. It has been there for several centuries, ever since a thief tried to steal the jewels from the Madonna on the high altar. The story goes that the Virgin grabbed his arm and held on so tightly it had to be cut off.

Because of its long nave, the church has excellent acoustics, and many concerts and recitals are given here. There is also a magnificent organ built in 1702.

Powder Gate
Prašná Brána

Ⓠ K4 **Ⓜ** Náměstí Republiky **Ⓜ** Náměstí Republiky **🚋** 6, 8, 15, 26 **Ⓒ** 10am-6pm daily (Mar & Oct: to 8pm; Apr-Sep: to 10pm)

Ⓦ muzeumprahy.cz

There has been a gate here since the 13th century, one of the 13 erstwhile entrances to the Old Town. In 1475, King Vladislav II laid the foundation stone of the New Tower, as it was then known. A coronation gift from the city council, the gate was modelled on Peter Parler's Old Town bridge tower built a century earlier. The gate had little defensive value; its rich sculptural decoration was intended to add prestige to the adjacent Royal Court. Building was halted eight years later when the king had to flee because of riots. On his return in 1485, he opted for the safety of Prague Castle. Royalty never again occupied the Royal Court.

←

Powder Gate, viewed from the Old Town

↑ The ornate Neo-Classical interior of the Estates Theatre

The gate acquired its present name when it was used to store gunpowder in the 17th century. The sculptural decoration, badly damaged during the Prussian occupation in 1757, was replaced in 1876.

Estates Theatre
Stavovské Divadlo

⊘ J5 ⚑ Ovocný trh 1 Ⓜ Můstek ⊙ For guided tours and performances only ⊚ narodni-divadlo.cz

Built by Count Nostitz in 1783, this opera theatre, originally know as the National Theatre, is one of Prague's finest examples of Neo-Classical elegance. It is a mecca for fans of Mozart. On 29 October 1787, the prodigious Austrian composer's opera *Don Giovanni* had its debut here with Mozart himself conducting. In 1834, the musical *Fidlovačka* premiered here;

one of the songs, "Where is my Home?", went on to become the Czech national anthem.

Celetná Street
Celetná Ulice

⊘ J4 Ⓜ Náměstí Republiky

One of the oldest streets in Prague, Celetná follows an old trading route from eastern Bohemia. Its name comes from the plaited bread rolls that were first baked here in the Middle Ages. It gained prestige in the 14th century as a section of the Royal Route, which linked two important royal seats – Municipal House and Prague Castle. The route's name originates from the coronation processions of the Bohemian kings and queens who passed along it.

Foundations of Gothic and Romanesque buildings can be seen in some of the cellars, but most

of the houses with their picturesque signs are Baroque remodellings.

At No 34, the House at the Black Madonna is a fine example of Cubist architecture. The building was designed by Josef Gočár in 1911.

There are several interesting shops, restaurants and museums located along the street. Museums include the Grévin Wax Museum and the Chocolate Museum.

 INSIDER TIP
Hostels

Prague has a relatively high concentration of budget-friendly hostels, some in very central locations. Dorm-room beds located just steps from the Old Town Square can go for as little as 300Kč per night.

↑ The imposing Jan Hus Monument in front of the pink-and-white Kinský Palace

Kinský Palace
Palác Kinských

⦿H4 ⌂Staroměstské náměstí 12
Ⓜ Staroměstská
Ⓒ 10am-6pm Tue-Sun
Ⓦ ngprague.cz

This lovely Rococo palace, designed by Kilian Ignaz Dientzenhofer, has a pretty pink-and-white stucco façade crowned with statues of the four elements by Ignaz Franz Platzer. It was bought from the Golz family in 1768 by František Kinský, an Imperial diplomat.

In 1948, Communist leader Klement Gottwald used the balcony to address a huge crowd of his party members – a key event in the crisis that led up to his coup d'état and the subsequent Communist government of Czechoslovakia that lasted for four decades. The National Gallery now

uses the palace for its temporary exhibitions.

Jan Hus Monument
Pomník Jana Husa

⦿H4 ⌂Staroměstské náměstí Ⓜ Staroměstská

At one end of the Old Town Square stands the massive monument to the religious reformer and central figure of the Bohemian Reformation, Jan Hus. Hus was burnt at the stake after being pronounced a heretic by the Council of Constance in 1415. The monument by Czech Art Nouveau sculptor Ladislav Šaloun was unveiled in 1915 on the 500th anniversary of his death. It shows two groups of people, one of victorious Hussite warriors, the other of Protestants forced into exile 200 years later, and

a young mother symbolizing national rebirth. The dominant central figure of Hus emphasizes the moral authority of the man who gave up his life rather than his beliefs.

Church of Our Lady Before Týn
Kostel Matky Boží Před Týnem

⦿J4 ⌂Staroměstské náměstí 14
Ⓜ Staroměstská, Můstek
Ⓒ 10am-1pm & 3-5pm Tue-Sat, 10am-noon Sun
Ⓦ prague.eu

Dominating the Old Town Square are the magnificent multiple steeples of this historic church. The present Gothic building was started in 1365 and soon became associated with the reform movement in Bohemia. From the early 15th century until 1620, Týn was the main Hussite church in Prague. The Hussite king, George of Poděbrady, took Utraquist communion here and had a gold chalice – the Utraquist symbol – mounted on the façade. After 1621, the chalice was melted down to become part of the statue of the Madonna that replaced it.

On the northern side of the church is a beautiful entrance portal (1390) decorated with scenes of Christ's

Passion. The dark interior has some notable features, including Gothic sculptures of *Calvary*, a pewter font (1414) and a 15th-century Gothic pulpit. Located behind the church is the Týn Courtyard, with its numerous architectural styles.

Carolinum

Karolinum

Q J5 **A** Ovocný trh 3
C 224 491 248 **M** Můstek
O For special exhibitions

At the core of the university founded by Charles IV in 1348 is the Carolinum. The original chapel, arcade and walls still survive, together with a fine oriel window, but in 1945, the courtyard was reconstructed in Gothic style. In the 15th and 16th centuries, the university played a leading role in the movement to reform the church. After the Bohemian defeat by Ferdinand II at the Battle of the White Mountain in 1620, the university was taken over by the Jesuits.

St Nicholas Cathedral

Chrám Sv. Mikuláše

Q H4 **A** Staroměstské náměstí **M** Staroměstská
O 10am–4pm daily (from noon Sun)
W svmikulas.cz

There has been a church here since the 12th century. It was the Old Town's parish church and meeting place until Týn Church was completed in the 14th century. After the Battle of the White Mountain in 1620, the church became part of a Benedictine monastery. The present church, designed by Kilian Ignaz Dientzenhofer, was completed in 1735. Its dramatic white façade is studded with statues by Antonín Braun. When in 1781 Emperor Joseph II closed all monasteries not engaged in socially useful activities, the church was stripped bare.

In World War I, the church was used by the troops of Prague's garrison. The colonel in charge took the opportunity to restore the church with the help of artists who might otherwise have been sent to the front line. The dome has frescoes of the lives of St Nicholas and St Benedict by Kosmas Damian Asam.

In the nave is a huge crown- shaped chandelier. At the end of the war, the church of St Nicholas was given to the Czechoslovak Hussite Church. The church is now a popular venue for live concerts and events.

St Nicholas Cathedral on the corner of Old Town Square
↓

↑ Baroque façade of the Church of St Gall

2,500 completed Lego models from the past 40 years. The museum is divided into 20 different themed areas, including ones dedicated to Indiana Jones, Harry Potter and Star Wars. There is also a playroom containing thousands of Lego bricks where anyone can build their own creations. Suitably inspired, few children fail to persuade parents to buy them a set or a bucket of bricks in the well-stocked gift shop.

Church of St Gall

Kostel Sv. Havla

Q J5 **A** Havelská
M Můstek **O** 11am–noon
Mon–Fri **W** tyn.cz

Dating from around 1265, this church was constructed to serve an autonomous German community located within the city walls known as Gall's Town (Havelské Město), which was merged with the Old Town in the 14th century.

Between 1722 and 1738, the church was given a Baroque facelift by Czech architect Pavel Bayer, who created a bold façade decorated with statues of saints by Baroque sculptor Matouš Jäckl. The monumental sculpture *Cavalry* by Ferdinand Brokoff can also be found in the church. Rich interior furnishings include paintings by the leading Baroque artist Karel Škréta, who is buried here.

Prague's best-known outdoor market has been held in Havelská Street since the Middle Ages; these days it sells an array of flowers, food and crafts.

Lego Museum

Muzeum Lega

Q H6 **A** Národní 362/31
M Národní Třída
O 9am–8pm daily
W muzeumlega.cz

Prague's vast Lego Museum is half Lego superstore, half private museum where visitors can view some

Church of St Martin in the Wall

Kostel Sv. Martina Ve Zdi

Q H6 **A** Martinská 8
M Národní třída, Můstek
⊞ 2, 9, 18, 22, 23
O 2–4pm Mon–Sat
W martinvezdi.eu

Built between 1178 and 1187, the south wall of this church became part of the city wall during the fortification of the Old Town in the 13th century, hence its name. It was the first church where bread and wine of the Eucharist, usually reserved for the clergy, was offered to the congregation. In 1784, the church was converted into flats, shops and a warehouse, but rebuilt in its original form in the early years of the 20th century.

Náprstek Museum

Náprstkovo Muzeum

🅿 G6 🏠 Betlémské náměstí 1 Ⓜ Národní třída, Staroměstská 🚊 2, 9, 18, 22, 23 🕙 10am-6pm Tue-Sun 🌐 nm.cz

Vojta Náprstek, an art patron and philanthropist, created this museum as a tribute to modern industry following a decade of exile in America after the 1848 revolution. On his return in 1862, inspired by London's Victorian museums, he began to form his collection. He created the Czech Industrial Museum by joining five older buildings together, and in the process virtually destroyed the Náprstek family brewery and home. He later turned to ethnography and the collection now consists of artifacts from Asian, African and Native American cultures, including weapons and ritual objects from the Aztecs, Toltecs and Maya peoples. The Náprstek is one of several buildings that form part of the National Museum. A number of temporary exhibitions on a range of subjects are also staged here.

Museum of Communism

Muzeum Komunismu

🅿 K4 🏠 V Celnici 4 Ⓜ Národní třída T 🚊 6, 8, 15, 26 🕙 9am-8pm daily 🌐 muzeumkomunismu.cz

This interesting museum explores how Communism affected every aspect of Prague society, such as sports, politics and home life, during the totalitarian regime that governed the country from the 1948 coup d'état through to 1989.

On display are original artifacts, from the museum's archive, alongside other rare items acquired from public and private collections. These include photos, propaganda material and film footage. There is also a re-creation of an interrogation room, complete with a spotlight and a typewriter. Some may enjoy the exhibitions for their nostalgic retro feel, others for the story it tells of one of Europe's most hardline Communist regimes.

EAT

Country Life

Pay for the food by weight at this long-established self-service health food café. There are two other locations in the city.

🅿 H5 🏠 Melantrichova 15 🕙 Sat 🌐 countrylife.cz

Havelská koruna

For a real taste of Czech cuisine, this basic self-service canteen plates up no-nonsense local staples.

🅿 H5 🏠 Havelská 21 🌐 havelska-koruna.cz

Café Slavia

Prague's most famous café where dissidents once met before the 1989 Velvet Revolution. There is live music every evening.

🅿 G7 🏠 Smetanovo nábřeží 2 🌐 cafeslavia.cz

Grand Café Orient

Located on the first floor of the House at the Black Madonna, this is quite possibly the only Cubist café in the world.

🅿 J4 🏠 Ovocný trh 19 🌐 grandcafeorient.cz

Clam-Gallas Palace
Clam-Gallasův Palác

Ⓠ H5 Ⓐ Husova 20
Ⓜ Staroměstská
**🚌 194 Ⓒ For concerts
and exhibitions only;
usually 10am–6pm
Tue–Sun 🌐 ahmp.cz**

This magnificent Baroque
palace, designed by
Viennese court architect
Johann Bernhard Fischer
von Erlach, was built in
1713–30 for the Supreme
Marshal of Bohemia,
Jan Gallas de Campo.
Its grand portals, each
flanked by two pairs of
Hercules sculpted by
Matthias Braun, give a
taste of what lies within.
The main staircase is
also decorated with
Braun statues, set off
by a ceiling fresco, *The
Triumph of God Helios*
by Carlo Carlone. Clam-
Gallas is currently
owned by
the Prague

City Archives, founded
in 1851. The building is
primarily used for a varied
programme of concerts,
exhibitions and other
social events.

Mariánské Square
Mariánské Náměstí

**Ⓠ H4 Ⓜ Staroměstská,
Můstek 🚌 194**

Two statues dominate
the square from the
corners of the imposing
New Town Hall (Nová
radnice), built in 1912.
One illustrates the story
of the long-lived Rabbi

> At the southern end of the square, a niche in the garden wall of the Clam-Gallas Palace houses a statue of the Vltava, depicted as a nymph pouring water from a jug.

Löw finally being caught
by the Angel of Death.
The other is the Iron Man,
a local ghost condemned
to roam the Old Town after
murdering his mistress.
At the southern end of
the square, a niche in the
garden wall of the Clam-
Gallas Palace houses a
statue of the Vltava, depic-
ted as a nymph pouring
water from a jug. The story
goes that an old soldier
once made the nymph
sole beneficiary of
his will.

Situated on the northern
side of the square, the
vast Municipal Library
hosts events, concerts,
theatre performances
and art exhibitions.

→

Interior decoration by artist Václav Vavřinec Reiner in the Church of St Giles

Church of St Giles

Kostel Sv. Jiljí

⦿H5 **⌂**Husova 8 **☏**724 320064 **Ⓜ**Národní třída **🚋**2, 9, 18, 22, 23 **⏰**Hours vary; call ahead

Despite the Gothic portal on the building's southern side, this church is essentially Baroque. Founded in 1371 on the site of a Romanesque church, the monumental Church of St Giles became a Hussite parish church in 1420. Following the Protestant defeat in 1620, Ferdinand II presented the church to the Dominicans, who built a huge friary on its southern side.

The vaults of the church are decorated with frescoes by the Baroque painter Václav Vavřinec Reiner, who is buried in the nave before the altar of St Vincent. The church's main fresco, a glorification of the Dominicans, shows St Dominic and his friars helping the Pope defend the Catholic Church from non-believers.

←

New Town Hall on Mariánské Square

Bethlehem Chapel

Betlémská Kaple

⦿H5 **⌂**Betlémské náměstí 4 **Ⓜ**Národní třída, Staroměstská **🚋**2, 9, 17, 18, 22, 23 **⏰**10am–6pm daily **🌐**bethlehemchapel.eu

The present "chapel" is a reconstruction of a medieval hall built between 1391 and 1394 by the followers of the radical preacher Jan Milíč z Kroměříže. The hall was used for preaching in the Czech language. Between 1402 and his excommunication in 1413, Jan Hus was a rector and preached in the chapel. Influenced by the teachings of the English religious reformer and theologian John Wycliffe (1330–84), Hus was dedicated to fighting against the corrupt practices of the church, arguing that the Scriptures should be the sole source of doctrine. After the Battle of the White Mountain in 1620, when Protestant worship was outlawed in Bohemia, the building was handed over to the Jesuits, who rebuilt it with six naves.

In 1786, the chapel was partially demolished; however, it was reconstructed to its original design in the 1950s by Czech modernist architect Jaroslav Fragner, who used fragments of preserved masonry as a reference.

Charles Street
Karlova Ulice

📍 G5 Ⓜ Staroměstská

Dating back to the 12th century, this narrow, winding street was part of the Royal Route, along which coronation processions passed on the way to Prague Castle. Many of the original Gothic and Renaissance houses remain, most converted into shops. A café at the House at the Golden Snake (No 18) was established in 1714 by an Armenian merchant, Deodatus Damajan, who handed out slanderous pamphlets from here. It is now a restaurant. Look out for At the Golden Well (No 3), which has a magnificent Baroque façade and stucco reliefs of various saints including St Roch and St Sebastian, who are believed to offer protection against plagues.

Colloredo-Mansfeld Palace
Colloredo-Mansfeldský palác

📍 G5 🏛 Karlova 2
Ⓜ Staroměstská 🚊 2, 17, 18 🚌 207 🕐 10am-6pm Tue-Sun 🌐 ghmp.cz

This magnificent 18th-century building is a fine example of Baroque and Rococo architectural styles. The interior has retained some original features, including wood floors, wallpaper and the

beautiful ceiling frescoes. The third floor displays temporary exhibitions of contemporary art.

Church of St Francis
Kostel Sv. Františka

📍 G5 🏛 Křižovnické náměstí 3 📞 221 108 255
Ⓜ Staroměstská 🚊 2, 17, 18 🚌 207 🕐 10am-7pm daily

This Baroque church was constructed between 1679 and 1685 by architects Gaudenzio Casanova and Domenico Canevalle, and was built on the remains of the original church of St Francis of Assisi, which dated back to 1270. A fresco of the Last Judgment by V V Reiner adorns the church's striking 40-m-(130-ft-) high cupola. The church is home to the city's

second oldest organ, an instrument that dates back to 1702. Excellent daily organ recitals take place here during the summer. The church is located on the north side of the small Knights of the Cross square (Křižovnické náměstí), which sits in front of the Old Town Bridge Tower and offers fine views across the Vltava. In the square stands a bronze Neo-Gothic statue of Charles IV.

Clementinum
Klementinum

📍 G5 🏛 Křižovnická 190, Karlova 1, Mariánské náměstí 5 Ⓜ Staroměstská 🚊 2, 17, 18
🕐 10am-6pm daily 🌐 klementinum.com

The Clementinum is a vast complex that was built between

the 16th and 18th centuries. In 1556, Emperor Ferdinand I invited the Jesuits to Prague to help bring the Czechs back into the Catholic fold. They established their head-quarters in the former Dominican monastery of St Clement, hence the name Clementinum. This became an effective rival to the Carolinum, the Utraquist university. In 1622, the two universities were merged. Between 1653 and 1723, the Clementinum expanded eastwards. Over 30 houses and three churches were pulled down to make way for the new complex. The Jesuits left in 1773 and the Clementinum was established as a library and observatory.

The Baroque library is housed in what is considered to be the most beautiful hall in the complex. The fresco ceilings by Jan Hiebl and the collection of historical globes are two of the highlights here.

Part of the observatory, the Astronomical Tower (1722) stands 68 m (223 ft) tall and has superb views of the city. Prague's first Jesuit church, the Church of the Holy Saviour (Kostel sv. Salvátora) was built here in 1601. Its façade, with seven

←

The Church of St Francis and its cupola

large statues of saints by Jan Bendl (1659), is dramatically lit up at night. Another church, devoted to St Clement, dates from 1715 and has one of the best Baroque interiors in Prague.

Classical music concerts occur regularly in the Mirror Chapel (Zrcadlová kaple), with its elegant interior and unique installation of mirrors. Regular guided tours include a visit to the Baroque library, Astronomical Tower and a brief look into the Mirror Chapel.

Smetana Museum
Muzeum Bedřicha Smetany

◉ G5 **Ⓜ** Novotného lávka 1 **Ⓜ** Staroměstská **🚋** 2, 17, 18 **◉** 10am-5pm Wed-Mon **Ⓦ** nm.cz

A former Neo-Renaissance waterworks building beside the Vltava has been turned into a memorial to Bedřich Smetana (1824–1884), the so-called father of Czech music. The museum contains documents, letters, scores and instruments detailing the composer's life and work. Smetana was a fervent patriot, and his music helped inspire the Czech national revival. Deaf towards the end of his life, he tragically never heard his cycle of symphonic poems, *Má Vlast* (My Country), being performed.

SHOP

Bric a Brac

This delightful junk shop is completely packed with local knick-knacks from down the ages, including some fascinating items from the Communist era.

◉ J4 **Ⓐ** Týnská 7

Granát Turnov

Bohemian garnet jewellery is produced in North Bohemia and Granát Turnov stocks the real thing.

◉ J3 **Ⓐ** Dlouhá 28 **Ⓦ** granat.cz

Manufaktura

The Czech Republic produces wonderful wooden toys as well as other decorative items made using natural materials. Manufaktura is the best place to source them.

◉ H5 **Ⓐ** Melantrichova 17 **Ⓐ** manufaktura.cz

A SHORT WALK
OLD TOWN

Distance 3 km (2 miles) **Nearest metro** Staroměstská
Time 35 minutes

Free of traffic (except for a few horse-drawn carriages) and ringed with colourful houses, Prague's Old Town Square (Staroměstské náměstí) ranks among the finest public spaces in any city. Little changed in over 100 years, Prague's fascinating history comes to life in the square's buildings. Streets like Celetná and Ovocný trh are also pedestrianized, making the quarter ideal for strolling. As you walk around look out for the decorative house signs.

Religious reformer Jan Hus is a symbol of integrity, and this monument to him brings together the highest and lowest points in Czech history.

STAROMĚSTSKÉ NÁMĚSTÍ

U Rotta is a former ironmonger's shop, decorated with colourful paintings by the 19th-century artist Mikuláš Aleš.

FINISH

START

The famous astronomical clock on the Old Town Hall draws a crowd of visitors every hour.

MALÉ NÁMĚSTÍ

ŽELEZNÁ

The carved Renaissance portal of the House At the Two Golden Bears is the finest of its kind in Prague.

The Štorch house has painted decoration based on designs by Mikuláš Aleš showing St Wenceslas on horseback.

↑ The elegant interior of the
Basilica of St James

Locator Map

STARÉ MĚSTO

The wooden Pietà
on the main altar
of the Basilica of
St James was made
in the 15th century.

An ornamental Baroque
plaque is the sign of the
House at the Black Sun
at No 8 Celetná Street.

The much-
restored Gothic
Powder Gate
stands at one of
the 13 original
11th-century
entryways into
the Old Town.

Týn
courtyard

JAKUBSKÁ

U PRAŠNÉ BRÁNY

ŠTUPARTSKÁ

CELETNÁ

The Art Nouveau
Municipal House
is a popular
concert venue.

OVOCNÝ TRH

Ovocný trh was Prague's
fruit market.

The Estates Theatre
featured in director Miloš
Forman's film Amadeus.

| 0 metres | 60 |
| 0 yards | 60 |

N ↑

JOSEFOV AND NORTHERN STARÉ MĚSTO

The Jewish Museum is your host in Josefov as you explore the mysterious synagogues and the wonderfully atmospheric Old Jewish Cemetery. This is also where you'll find a gathering of kosher restaurants, but there are very few other eateries and almost no hotels. The northern part of the Old Town is a quieter affair than the area around the Old Town Square, providing a more tranquil and authentically Prague experience.

Stunning Moorish interior of the Spanish Synagogue ↓

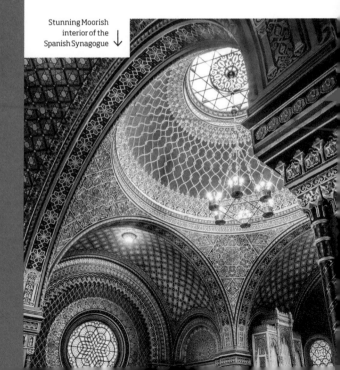

↑ Some of the thousands of gravestones at the Old Jewish Cemetery

JEWISH MUSEUM

📍 H3 🏠 Ticket Centre: Maiselova 15 Ⓜ Staroměstská
🚋 2, 17, 18 🚌 194, 207 🕐 All sites: 9am–6pm Sun–Fri
(Nov–Mar: to 4:30pm) 🌐 jewishmuseum.cz

The Jewish Museum's collection of Judaic art is perhaps the world's largest, with 40,000 artifacts and 100,000 books, while other exhibits present the lives and history of the Jewish people in Bohemia and Moravia.

> ### TICKETS
>
> All of the museum sites are covered by a single ticket, which is available from the ticket office, the synagogues (except the Maisel) or online. It is best to arrive early at the Old Jewish Cemetery to avoid the crowds in this confined space.

The museum consists of four historical synagogues, the Old Jewish Cemetery, the Ceremonial Hall and the Robert Guttman Gallery. The Maisel Synagogue, with its exhibitions on Jewish life in Prague, is a good introduction to the museum. The Spanish Synagogue has an intricately decorated, mysterious interior which contains yet more intriguing exhibitions, while the Pinkas Synagogue is possibly the most memorable, with the names of 80,000 Czech Jews who died in the Holocaust inscribed on the walls. The Old Jewish Cemetery is a wonderfully atmospheric place with its crooked gravestones and their Hebrew inscrip-tions. Nearby, the Klausen Synagogue has an exhibition on Jewish rituals and the Ceremonial Hall, next door, contains an illuminating exhibition on death and Jewish funerals. Finally, the Robert Guttman Gallery hosts temporary exhibitions from the museum's collection.

EXPLORING THE JEWISH MUSEUM

EXPERIENCE Josefov and Northern Staré Město

Spanish Synagogue

Španělská Synagoga

🔲 **Vězeňská 1, Dušní 12**

Prague's first synagogue, known as the Old School (Stará škola), once stood on this site. In the 11th century, the Old School was the centre of the community of Jews of the eastern rite, who lived strictly apart from Jews of the western rite, who were concentrated round the Old-New Synagogue. The present building dates from the second half of the 19th century. The exterior and interior are both pseudo-Moorish in appearance. The rich stucco decorations on the walls and vaults are reminiscent of the Alhambra in Spain, hence the name. Once closed to the public, the Spanish Synagogue now houses a permanent exhibition dedicated to the history of the Jews from emancipation to the present.

Robert Guttmann Gallery

Galerie Robertu Guttmannovi palác

🔲 **U Staré školy 3**

Named after Jewish naïve artist Robert Guttman (1880-1942), this gallery displays temporary exhibitions using pieces from the Jewish Museum's collection. The main focus of the displays is on Jewish life in Bohemia and Moravia throughout history, including the persecution of the Jews in World War II. Exhibits have included works by 19th- and early 20th-century local Jewish artists, as well as modern art.

Pinkas Synagogue

Pinkasova Synagoga

🔲 **Široká 3**

The synagogue was founded in 1479 by Rabbi Pinkas and enlarged in 1535 by his great-nephew Aaron Meshulam Horowitz. It has been rebuilt many times over the centuries. Excavations have turned up fascinating relics of life in the medieval ghetto, including a *mikva*, or ritual bath. The core of the present building is a hall with Gothic vaulting. The gallery for women was added in the early 17th century. The synagogue now serves as a memorial to all the Jewish Czechoslovak citizens who were imprisoned in Terezín concentration camp, which was located 70 km (43 miles) north of Prague. It was this camp that the Nazis used for propaganda purposes, duping the Red Cross into writing favourable reports, but the reality was very different. By the end of World War II, most of the Jews had been sent to the death camps. The names of the 77,297 who did not return are inscribed on the synagogue walls. The building houses a moving exhibition of children's drawings from the Terezín concentration camp.

Maisel Synagogue

Maiselova Synagoga
Smetany

🔲 **Maiselova 10**

Rudolf II gave mayor Mordechai Maisel permission to build his private synagogue here in the late 16th century, in gratitude for the Jewish mayor's financial help in Bohemia's war against the Turks. It was the most richly decorated in the city. The original building was a victim of the fire that devastated the Jewish Town in 1689 and a new synagogue was built in its place. Its present crenellated, Gothic appearance dates from the start of the 20th century. Inside is a wonderful collection of Torah crowns, shields and finials. Crowns and finials were used to decorate the rollers on which the text of the Torah (the five books of Moses) was kept. The shields were hung over the mantle that was draped over the Torah. There are also objects such as wedding plates, lamps and candlesticks. By a tragic irony, nearly all these Jewish treasures were brought to Prague by the Nazis from synagogues throughout Bohemia and Moravia with the intention of founding a museum of a vanished people.

Klausen Synagogue
Klausová Synagoga

🏛 U Starého hřbitova

Before the fire of 1689, this site was occupied by a number of small Jewish schools and prayer houses known as *klausen*. The name was preserved in the Klausen Synagogue, built on the ruins and completed in 1694. The High Baroque structure has a fine barrel-vaulted interior with rich stucco decorations. It now houses a collection of Torah pointers, Hebrew manuscripts and prints. There is also an exhibition of Jewish traditions and customs, tracing the history of the Jews in Central Europe back to the early Middle Ages. Many exhibits relate to famous figures in the city's Jewish community including the 16th-century Rabbi Löw, who founded a *yeshivah* (Talmudic school) which used to occupy a 16th-century building on this site.

Ceremonial Hall
Obřadní síň

🏛 U Starého hřbitova 3a

Adjoining the Klausen Synagogue is a building that looks like a tiny medieval castle. The Ceremonial Hall, constructed in the early 1900s in striking mock Romanesque fashion, was home to the Jewish community's Burial Society. The exhibits housed inside detail the complex Jewish rituals for preparing the dead for the grave.

Old Jewish Cemetery
Starý Židovský Hřbitov

🏛 Široká 3 (main entrance)

The sight of hundreds of graves, their leaning headstones crumbling on top of each other, is a moving and unforgettable experience. This remarkable site was, for over 300 years, the only burial ground permitted to Jews. Founded in 1478, it was slightly enlarged over the years but still basically corresponds to its medieval size. Because of the lack of space, people had to be buried on top of each other, up to 12 layers deep. There is no definite record of the number of burial sites here, although estimates put it at about 100,000 graves. To appreciate the depth of the graveyard, compare the gravestones' height with that of the street level on U Starého hřbitova. The oldest headstone in the cemetery dates from 1439 and the final burial, of Moses Beck, took place in 1787. The most visited grave is that of Rabbi Löw (1520–1609). Visitors place hundreds of pebbles and wishes on his grave as a mark of respect. Also of note is the highly decorated tombstone marking the grave of Hendl Bassevi (1628), which was built for the beautiful wife of Prague's first Jewish nobleman, and the tomb of astronomer David Gans (1541–1613), marked with a Star of David and a goose, after his faith and name. Embedded in the cemetery's eastern wall are fragments of Gothic tombstones brought here from an older Jewish cemetery, which was found in 1866 in Vladislavova Street.

← Jewish exhibits on display in the Klausen Synagogue

OLD-NEW SYNAGOGUE

STARONOVÁ SYNAGOGA

⊞H3 ⌂Červená 2 ⓂStaroměstská ⬚2, 17, 18 to Staroměstská, 17 to Law Faculty (Právnická fakulta) ⬚194, 207 ⏲9am–6pm Sun–Fri (Nov–Mar: to 5pm) ⬚Jewish holidays ⬚synagogue.cz

Built around 1270, this is the oldest synagogue in Europe and one of the earliest Gothic buildings in Prague. The interior, with its antique furnishings, looks much as it did in the 15th century.

The synagogue has survived fires, the slum clearances of the 19th century and many Jewish pogroms. Residents of the Jewish Quarter have often had to seek refuge within its walls and today it is still the religious centre for Prague's Jews. Its name may come from the fact that another synagogue was built after this one, taking the title "new", but which was later destroyed. Legend has it that the stones will eventually have to be returned to Jerusalem whence they came.

↑ The Ark is the holiest place in the synagogue and holds the sacred scrolls of the Torah

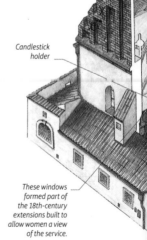

Candlestick holder

These windows formed part of the 18th-century extensions built to allow women a view of the service.

Cross-section of the Gothic ↑ Old-New Synagogue

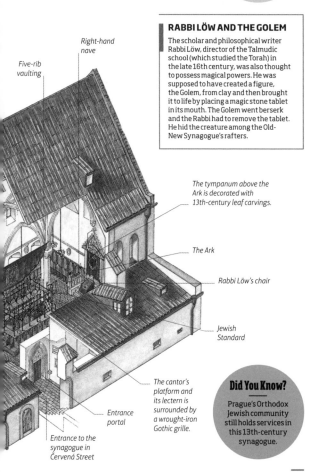

Five-rib vaulting

Right-hand nave

RABBI LÖW AND THE GOLEM

The scholar and philosophical writer Rabbi Löw, director of the Talmudic school (which studied the Torah) in the late 16th century, was also thought to possess magical powers. He was supposed to have created a figure, the Golem, from clay and then brought it to life by placing a magic stone tablet in its mouth. The Golem went berserk and the Rabbi had to remove the tablet. He hid the creature among the Old-New Synagogue's rafters.

The tympanum above the Ark is decorated with 13th-century leaf carvings.

The Ark

Rabbi Löw's chair

Jewish Standard

The cantor's platform and its lectern is surrounded by a wrought-iron Gothic grille.

Entrance portal

Entrance to the synagogue in Červená Street

Did You Know?

Prague's Orthodox Jewish community still holds services in this 13th-century synagogue.

↑ The splendid façade of the Rudolfinum lit up at night

EXPERIENCE MORE

Rudolfinum

📍 G3 🏛 Alšovo nábřeží 12 Ⓜ Staroměstská 🚊 2, 17, 18 🚌 194, 207 🕐 10am–6pm Tue–Sun (to 8pm Thu) 🌐 ceskafilharmonie.cz

As well as being home to the Czech Philharmonic Orchestra, the Rudolfinum is one of the most impressive landmarks on the Old Town bank of the Vltava. Many of the major concerts of the Prague Spring International Music Festival are held here. There are several concert halls located within the complex, and the sumptuous Dvořák Hall is one of the finest creations of 19th-century Czech architecture. The Rudolfinum was built between 1876 and 1884 to a design by architects Josef Zítek and Josef Schulz, and named in honour of Crown Prince Rudolph of Habsburg. Like the National Theatre, it is an outstanding example of Czech Neo-Renaissance style. The curving balustrade is decorated with statues of distinguished Czech, Austrian and German composers and artists. Also known as the House of Artists (Dům umělců), the building houses the Galerie Rudolfinum, a collection of modern art. Between 1919 and 1941, and for a brief period after World War II, the Rudolfinum was the seat of the Czechoslovak parliament.

High Synagogue

Vysoká Synagoga

📍 H3 🏛 Červená 2 Ⓜ Staroměstská 🚊 2, 17, 18 🚌 194, 207 🕐 For services only 🌐 kehilaprag.cz

Like the Jewish Town Hall, the building of the High Synagogue was financed by Mordechai Maisel, mayor of the Jewish Town, in the 1570s. Originally, the two buildings formed a single complex and to facilitate communication with the Jewish Town Hall, the main hall of the synagogue was on the first floor. It was not until the 19th century that the adjoined buildings were separated and the synagogue was given a staircase and street entrance. Visitors can still see the original Renaissance vaulting and stucco decoration.

St Agnes of Bohemia Convent

Klášter Sv. Anežky Ceské

📍 J2 🏛 U Milosrdných 17 Ⓜ Náměstí Republiky, Staroměstská 🚊 6, 8, 15, 17, 26 🚌 207 🕐 10am–6pm Tue–Sun; gardens: 9am–6pm (Nov–Mar: to 4pm) 🌐 ngprague.cz

Dating from around 1230, this convent was founded by the Přemyslid princess St Agnes of Bohemia – who was not canonized until 1989 – along with her brother King Wenceslas I. The convent, one of the very first Gothic buildings in Bohemia, was abolished in 1782 and used as storage space and to house the poor, later falling into disrepair. Following a painstaking restoration in the 1960s, it has recovered much of its original appearance and is now used by the National Gallery to display a large collection of medieval painting and sculpture from Bohemia and Central Europe, dating from between the 13th and 16th centuries.

The permanent exhibition is housed on the first floor of the old convent in a long gallery and smaller rooms around the cloister. Top billing among the artworks goes to the votive panel of Archbishop Jan Očko of Vlašim, painted around 1370 by an anonymous artist. It shows Charles IV kneeling before the Virgin in Heaven. *The Annunciation of Our Lady* was painted around 1350 by the renowned Master of the Vyšší Brod Altar and is one of the oldest and finest works in the museum. The 700-year-old *Strakonice Madonna* evokes the Classical French sculpture found in such places as Reims Cathedral, while the *Variant of the Krumlov Madonna*, dating from around 1400, is a touching image of the mother and her child.

Jewish Town Hall
Židovská Radnice

Ⓠ H4 **🏠 Maiselova 18**
📞 224 800 849
Ⓜ Staroměstská
🚊 2, 17, 18 **🚌 194, 207**
🕐 To the public

The core of this attractive blue-and-white building is the original Jewish Town Hall, built between 1570 and 1577 by architect Panacius Roder at the expense of the immensely rich mayor, Mordechai Maisel.

In 1763, it acquired a new appearance in the flowery style of the Late Baroque. The latest alterations date from 1908, when the southern wing was enlarged. The building is one of the few monuments that survived far-reaching "sanitation" of this medieval part of Prague at the beginning of the 20th century.

On the roof stands a small wooden clock tower with a distinctive green steeple. Sitting on one of the gables there is another clock. Interestingly, this one has Hebrew figures and, because the language reads from right to left, hands that turn in an anticlockwise direction. The Town Hall is now the seat of the Council of Jewish Religious Communities in Czechia.

UPM (Museum of Decorative Arts)
Uměleckoprůmyslové Muzeum

Ⓠ G3 **🏠 17 listopadu 2**
Ⓜ Staroměstská **🚊 2, 17, 18** **🚌 207** **🕐 10am–6pm Tue–Sun (to 7pm Tue)**
🌐 upm.cz

For a number of years after its foundation in 1885, the museum's collections were housed in the Rudolfinum. The present building, designed by Josef Schulz in French Neo-Renaissance style, was completed in 1901. The museum's glass collection is one of the largest in the world, but only a fraction of it is ever on display. Pride of place goes to the Bohemian glass, of which there are many fine Baroque and 19th- and 20th-century pieces. Medieval and Venetian Renaissance glass are also well represented.

Among the permanent exhibitions of other crafts are Meissen porcelain, the Gobelin tapestries and displays covering fashion, textiles, photography and printing. On the mezzanine floor are halls for temporary exhibitions and an extensive art library housing more than 190,000 publications. In 2017, a third floor of exhibition space was added, and the relaxation garden, previously not accessible to the public, was opened.

Church of St Castullus

Kostel Sv. Haštala

⊞ J3 **⌂ Haštalské námestí** **🚋 6, 8, 15, 26** **🚌 207** **🕐 Times vary**

This peaceful little corner of Prague takes the name Haštal from the parish church of St Castullus. One of the finest Gothic buildings in Prague, the church was erected on the site of an older Romanesque structure in the 14th century. Much of the church had to be rebuilt after the fire of 1689, but the double nave on the north side survived. The interior furnishings are mainly Baroque, though there are remains of wall paintings from about 1375 in the sacristy and a metal font decorated with figures dating from about 1650. Standing in the Gothic nave is an impressive sculptural group depicting *Calvary* (1716) from the workshop of Ferdinand Maxmilián Brokoff.

Cubist Houses

Kubistické Domy

⊞ H3 **⌂ Eliška Krásnohorské, 10–14** **Ⓜ Staroměstská** **🚋 2, 17, 18** **🚌 207** **🕐 To the public**

The rebuilding of the city's old Jewish Quarter at the turn of the 20th century gave Prague's architects scope to experiment with many new styles. Most of the blocks in the area are covered with flowing Art Nouveau decoration, but on the corner of Bílkova and Eliška Krásnohorské, there is a plain façade with a few simple repeated geometrical shapes. Cubist architecture did not really catch on in the rest of Europe, but was very popular with the avant-garde in Bohemia and Austria before and after World War I. This block was built for a cooperative of teachers in 1919–21. At No 7 Eliška Krásnohorské, you can see the influence of Cubism in the curiously geometric figures supporting the windows. Another interesting classic Cubist building is the House at the Black Madonna in Celetná Street.

Church of the Holy Ghost

Kostel Sv. Ducha

⊞ H3 **⌂ Eliška Krásnohorské** **Ⓜ Staroměstská** **🚋 2, 17, 18** **🚌 207** **🕐 Only for services**

This church stands on the narrow strip of Christian

soil that once separated the two Jewish communities of the Middle Ages – the eastern and western rites. Built in the 14th century, the Gothic church was originally part of a convent of Benedictine nuns, but the convent was destroyed in 1420 during the Hussite Wars and not rebuilt. Though the church was badly damaged in the Old Town fire of 1689, the exterior preserves the original Gothic buttresses and high windows. The vault of the nave, however, was rebuilt in Baroque style. The high altar dates from 1760, and there is an altar painting of *St Joseph* by Jan Jiří Heintsch (c 1647–1712). In front of the church stands a Baroque stone statue of St John Nepomuk distributing alms (1727) by the Baroque sculptor Ferdinand Maxmilián Brokoff.

Church of St Simon and St Jude
Kostel Sv. Šimona
A Judy
📍 H3 ⬛ Dušní/U milosrdných
Ⓜ Staroměstská 🚊 2, 17, 18 🚌 207 🌐 fok.cz

Members of the Bohemian Brethren built this church

The Gothic exterior of the church of the Holy Ghost

with its high, late-Gothic windows between 1615 and 1620. Founded in the mid-15th century, the Brethren agreed with the Hussite Utraquists in directing the congregation to receive both bread and wine at Holy Communion.

After the Battle of the White Mountain, the Brethren were expelled from the Holy Roman Empire. The church was then given to a Catholic order, the Brothers of

Mercy, becoming part of a monastery and hospital. In the 18th century, it was adapted in High Baroque style and an organ was installed, on which both Mozart and Haydn were known to have played.

It was here that anaesthesia was first applied in Europe (1847) and the complex continues to serve as a hospital – the Na Františku. The church is now used as a venue for concerts.

EAT

Krčma
A medieval-themed tavern, Krčma offers reasonably priced food, draft beer and lots of low-lit ambience.

📍 H4 ⬛ Kostečná 4
🌐 krcma.cz

V Kolkovně
Wash down Czech pub favourites such as pork knuckle and goulash with beer at this more upmarket tavern.

📍 H3 ⬛ V kolkovně 8
🌐 vkolkovne.cz

Lokál
Well-prepared pub food and Urquell beer are the double act at this minimalist inn.

📍 J3 ⬛ Dlouhá 33
🌐 ambi.cz

King Solomon
This top-notch kosher restaurant plates up international and traditional Jewish cuisine. There is also a carefully selected wine list.

📍 H4 ⬛ Široká 8 🕐 Fri
🌐 kosher.cz

A SHORT WALK

JEWISH QUARTER

Distance 2.5 km (1.6 miles) **Nearest metro** Staroměstská **Time** 25 minutes

Though the old ghetto has disappeared, much of the area's fascinating history is preserved in the synagogues around the Old Jewish Cemetery, while the newer streets are lined with many delightful Art Nouveau buildings. The old lanes to the east of the former ghetto lead to the quiet haven of St Agnes's Convent, beautifully restored as a branch of the National Gallery.

↑ Gravestones crowded together in the Old Jewish Cemetery

The Cubist Houses, based on the ideas of Cubism, represent one of the many new architectural styles used in the rebuilding of the old Jewish Quarter.

The Gothic Old-New Synagogue, with its distinctive crenellated gable, has been a house of prayer for over 700 years.

START

FINISH

The interior of the High Synagogue has splendid Renaissance vaulting.

The exhibits of the Jewish Museum at the Klausen Synagogue include an alms box, dating from about 800.

Stained-glass panels on the staircase depict the crafts represented in the wide-ranging collection of the UPM.

The walls of the Pinkas Synagogue are a moving memorial to the Czech Jews killed in the Holocaust.

The 16th-century Jewish Town Hall still serves the Czech Jewish community.

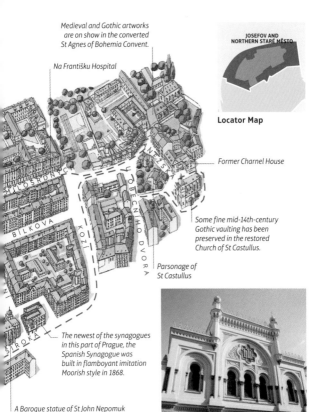

Medieval and Gothic artworks are on show in the converted St Agnes of Bohemia Convent.

Na Františku Hospital

JOSEFOV AND NORTHERN STARÉ MĚSTO

Locator Map

Former Charnel House

Some fine mid-14th-century Gothic vaulting has been preserved in the restored Church of St Castullus.

Parsonage of St Castullus

MILOSRDNÝCH

BILKOVA

KOZÍ

OBECNIHO DVORA

U OBECNÍHO DVORA

ŠIROKÁ

The newest of the synagogues in this part of Prague, the Spanish Synagogue was built in flamboyant imitation Moorish style in 1868.

A Baroque statue of St John Nepomuk by Ferdinand Maxmilián Brokoff (1727) stands in front of the Church of the Holy Ghost.

0 metres 50

0 yards 50

N

↑ The Moorish-inspired exterior of the Spanish Synagogue

PRAGUE CASTLE AND HRADČANY

History and art fans will love Hradčany, the smallest of Prague's historical districts, as well as Prague Castle. Around it are arranged huge Baroque palaces that house various ministries and some of the National Gallery. Outside the confines of the Hrad, the rest of the neighbourhood is made up of Nový Svět, an enchanting tangle of cobbled lanes which gives some impression of what all of the Left Bank was like before the devastating fire of 1541.

↓ Small houses built into the castle wall at Golden Lane

← The west nave completed by Joseph Mocker

← The Gothic splendour of St Vitus's spires, towering above the surrounding houses

ST VITUS'S CATHEDRAL
KATEDRÁLA SV. VÍTA, VÁCLAVA A VOJTĚCHA

📍D3 🏰Prague Castle, third courtyard Ⓜ️Hradčanská, Malostranská 🚋22 to Prague Castle (Pražský hrad) 🕐Cathedral: 9am–5pm Mon–Sat, noon–5pm Sun (except during services); Great South Tower: 10am–5pm daily (Apr–Oct: to 6pm) 🌐hrad.cz

The spectacular Gothic St Vitus's Cathedral is an unmissable sight, not least because its dominant position on Hradčany hill means its spires can be seen from almost every vantage point in the city. The cathedral's beautiful stained-glass windows and gargoyles are worth seeing up close.

Prince Wenceslas first built a rotunda here on a pagan worship site and dedicated it to St Vitus (svatý Vít), a Roman saint. Work began on the city's most distinctive landmark in 1344 on the orders of John of Luxembourg. The first archi-tect was the Frenchman Matthew of Arras. He died shortly thereafter and Charles IV hired Swabian Peter Parler to take over. His masons' lodge worked on the building until the Hussite Wars when work stopped and, remarkably, construc-tion was only finally completed in 1929 by 19th- and 20th-century architects and artists. The cathedral houses the crown jewels and some fine works of art.

 INSIDER TIP
Visit for Free

The western entrance areas of St Vitus's can be visited for free – you'll see about a quarter of the building. Admission is charged for all other areas.

Exploring St Vitus's Cathedral

A walk around St Vitus's takes you back through a thousand years of history. Go in through the west portal to see some of the best elements of the modern, Neo-Gothic style and continue past a succession of side chapels to catch glimpses of religious artifacts, saintly relics and works of art from Renaissance paintings to modern statuary. Allow plenty of time to visit the richly decorated, jewel-encrusted St Wenceslas Chapel before you leave.

The Renaissance Great South Tower is capped with a Baroque "helmet".

Bronze weathercock

Twin west spires

The Rose Window, located above the portals, was designed by František Kysela in 1925–7 and depicts scenes from the biblical story of the creation.

Main entrance

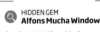

HIDDEN GEM
Alfons Mucha Window

Czech artist Alfons Mucha created the notable Art Nouveau window of the Slavic saints for the New Archbishops Chapel. Despite appearances, the glass is painted not stained.

287

steps lead to the top of the Great South Tower, where there are great views of the city.

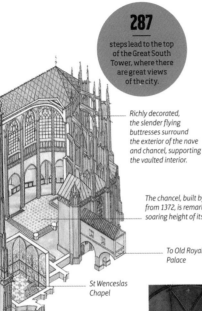

Richly decorated, the slender flying buttresses surround the exterior of the nave and chancel, supporting the vaulted interior.

The chancel, built by Peter Parler from 1372, is remarkable for the soaring height of its vault.

To Old Royal Palace

St Wenceslas Chapel

Golden Portal

Gothic vaulting

① The walls of the St Wenceslas Chapel are covered with Gothic frescoes, depicting scenes from the Bible and the life of the saint interspersed with fine gilding. The chapel houses the saint's tomb and the crown jewels.

② Light floods into the chancel through colourful stained-glass-windows.

③ Standing on the roof of the cathedral is this bronze weathercock.

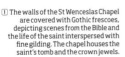

LORETA

📍B4 🏠Loretánské náměstí 7, Hradčany 🚋 22, 25 to Pohořelec
🕐Apr–Oct: 9am–5pm daily; Nov–Mar: 9:30am–4pm daily 🌐loreta.cz

The onion-domed white towers of this Baroque 17th-century church complex are like something out of a fairy tale. At its heart is its claim to fame and most proud possession: a replica of the original Santa Casa in Loreto, Italy.

Ever since its construction in 1626, the Loreta has been an important place of pilgrimage. It was commissioned by Kateřina of Lobkowicz, a Czech aristocrat who was very keen to promote the legend of the Santa Casa of Loreto. The Santa Casa was enclosed by cloisters in 1661, and a Baroque façade 60 years later by Christoph and Kilian Ignaz Dientzenhofer. The grandiose design and miraculous stories about the Loreto were part of Ferdinand II's campaign to recatholicize the Czechs.

LEGEND OF THE SANTA CASA

The original Santa Casa was the house in Nazareth in which the Archangel Gabriel is believed to have announced to the Virgin Mary that she would conceive the Son of God. In the 13th century, the Greek Angeli family moved the house to the small Italian town of Loreto. After the Protestants' defeat in 1620, Catholics promoted the legend, and 50 replicas of the Italian Loreto emerged all over Europe, including in Bohemia and Moravia. The 17th-century Prague site is the grandest and is believed to be the truest representation of the original structure.

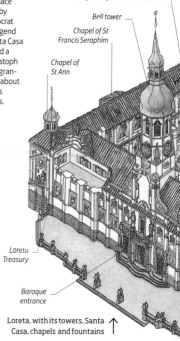

Fountain decorated with a sculpture of the Resurrection

Bell tower

Chapel of St Francis Seraphim

Chapel of St Ann

Loreta Treasury

Baroque entrance

Loreta, with its towers, Santa Casa, chapels and fountains ↑

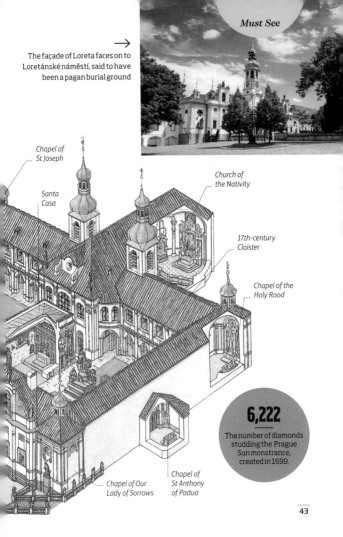

The façade of Loreta faces on to Loretánské náměstí, said to have been a pagan burial ground →

Chapel of St Joseph

Santa Casa

Church of the Nativity

17th-century Cloister

Chapel of the Holy Rood

Chapel of Our Lady of Sorrows

Chapel of St Anthony of Padua

6,222

The number of diamonds studding the Prague Sun monstrance, created in 1699.

STRAHOV MONASTERY
STRAHOVSKÝ KLÁŠTER

📍 B5 🏠 Strahovské nádvoří 1 🚋 22, 25 to Pohořelec 🕐 9am–noon & 1–5pm daily 🌐 strahovskyklaster.cz

Strahov houses the nation's oldest books in the Strahov Library while still functioning as a monastery. The Theological Hall is a highlight, with its frescoes, astronomical globes and the statue of St John the Evangelist.

Founded in 1140 by an austere religious order, the Premonstratensians, Strahov was destroyed by fire in 1258 and rebuilt in the Gothic style, with later Baroque additions. Its famous library, in the theological and philosophical halls, is over 800 years old, holds around 200,000 volumes and, despite being ransacked by many invading armies, is one of the finest in Bohemia. On display are books, pictures, ornate gospels and Bibles.

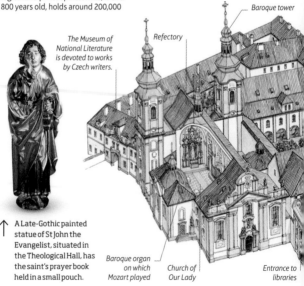

Baroque tower

The Museum of National Literature is devoted to works by Czech writers.

Refectory

↑ A Late-Gothic painted statue of St John the Evangelist, situated in the Theological Hall, has the saint's prayer book held in a small pouch.

Baroque organ on which Mozart played

Church of Our Lady

Entrance to libraries

① The ceiling fresco in the Philosophical Hall depicts the *Struggle of Mankind to Know Real History* by Franz Maulbertsch. The hall was built in 1782 to hold the Baroque bookcases and their valuable books from a dissolved monastery near Louka, in Moravia.

② Dazzling with opulence, the interior of the Baroque Church of Our Lady is highly decorated with magnificent furnishings and gilded Rococo statues.

③ One of the 17th-century astronomical globes by William Blaeu that line the Theological Hall. The stucco and wall paintings relate to librarianship.

Theological Hall

Philosophical Hall

↑ The Strahov Monastery complex, including the Philosophical Hall and Church of Our Lady

STRAHOV MONASTERY EXHIBITS

Josef II dissolved most local monasteries in 1783, sparing Strahov on the condi-tion that the monks conduct research at their library. Today, the majority of the research involves paper preservation. On display are old books, pic-tures, ornate gospels and miniature Bibles.

OLD ROYAL PALACE
STARÝ KRÁLOVSKÝ PALÁC

📍 D3 🏰 Prague Castle, third courtyard Ⓜ Hradčanská, up K Brusce, then through the Royal Garden; Malostranská, left up Klárov, then up Old Castle Steps 🚊 22 to Prague Castle (Pražský hrad) 🕐 Apr–Oct: 9am–5pm daily; Nov–Mar: 9am–4pm daily; last adm: 1hr before closing 🌐 hrad.cz

From the time Prague Castle was first fortified in stone in the 11th century, the palace was the seat of Bohemian princes. The building consists of three different architectural layers.

A Romanesque palace built by Soběslav I around 1135 forms the cellars of the present building. Přemysl Otakar II and Charles IV then added their own palaces above this in the 13th and 14th centuries, while the top floor, built for Vladislav Jagiello, contains the massive Gothic Vladislav Hall. This vast and opulent hall is the highlight of the palace. It has superb rib vaulting and is lit by large windows that heralded the advent of the Renaissance in Bohemia. The room was used not only for state functions, but also for jousting. The architect's unusual staircase design, with gently sloping steps, allowed knights to enter the hall without having to dismount from their horses. The adjacent Ludvík Wing was, in 1618, the scene of the famous defenestration which led to the outbreak of the Thirty Years' War. During the period of Habsburg rule, the palace housed government offices, courts and the old Bohemian Diet (parliament).

DEFENESTRATION OF 1618

On 23 May 1618, more than 100 Protestant nobles stormed the palace to protest against the succession to the throne of the intolerant Habsburg Archduke Ferdinand. The nobles threw the two Catholic Governors appointed by Ferdinand and their secretary out of the eastern window. Protestants said the men survived the 15 m (50 ft) fall by landing in a dung heap, while Catholics claimed they were saved by the intervention of angels. This event is often sited as the spark that began the Thirty Years' War.

Did You Know?

An overhead passage from the Old Royal Palace leads to the Royal Oratory in St Vitus's Cathedral.

→ Gothic Vladislav Hall's magnificent rib vaulting, designed by Benedikt Ried

1

1 Designed in Gothic and Renaissance styles, the grand Old Royal Palace dates from the 11th century. It has been used as a site for coronations and jousting tournaments, and, since the First Republic, the country's presidents have been ceremoniously sworn in here.

2 With its wide and gently sloping steps and Gothic rib vaulted ceiling, the Riders' Staircase permitted knights on horseback to make a grand entrance to Vladislav Hall for indoor jousting competitions.

3 The ceiling and walls of the New Land Rolls room is decorated with the crests of clerks who tracked property ownership and court decisions from 1561 to 1774.

2

3

EXPERIENCE MORE

Dalibor Tower
Daliborka

📍E2 🏛Prague Castle,
Zlatá ulička
Ⓜ Malostranská
🚌2, 12, 15, 18, 20, 22
🕐9am–5pm daily (Nov–
Mar: to 4pm) 🌐hrad.cz

This 15th-century tower
with a conical roof was
part of the fortifications
built by King Vladislav
Jagiello, whose coat of
arms can be seen on
the outer wall. The tower
also served as a prison
and is named after its
first inmate, Dalibor of
Kozojed, a young knight
sentenced to death for
harbouring outlawed serfs.
While awaiting execution,
he was kept in a dungeon,
into which he had to be
lowered through a hole
in the floor.

According to legend,
while in prison he learnt
to play the violin. People
sympathetic to his plight
came to listen to his
playing and provided him
with food and drink, which
they lowered on a rope
from a window – prisoners
were often left to starve
to death. The story was
used by Bedřich Smetana
in his opera *Dalibor*. The
tower ceased to serve as
a prison in 1781. Visitors
can see part of the
old prison.

Golden Lane
Zlatá Ulička

📍E3 Ⓜ Malostranská,
Hradčanská 🚌22

Named after the goldsmiths
who lived here in the 17th
century, this short, narrow
street is one of the most
picturesque in Prague. The
brightly painted houses
were built right into the
arches of the castle walls in
the late 1500s for Rudolph
II's castle guards. A century
later, the goldsmiths moved
in and modified the buildings. But by the 19th century,
the area had turned into a
slum. In the 1950s, the ten-
ants were moved out and
the area restored to something like its original state.
The house at No 20 is the
oldest and the least altered
in appearance. Most of the
houses were converted
into shops selling books,
Bohemian glass and
other souvenirs.

Powder Tower
Prašná Věž

📍D3 🏛Prague Castle,
Vikářská Ⓜ Malostranská,
Hradčanská 🚌22
🕐9am–5pm daily (Nov–
Mar: to 4pm) 🌐hrad.cz

A tower was built here
in about 1496 by the King
Vladislav II's architect
Benedikt Ried as a cannon
bastion overlooking the
Stag Moat. The original
was destroyed in the fire
of 1541, but it was rebuilt
as the home and work-
shop of gunsmith and
bell founder Tomáš Jaroš,
who made the 18-tonne
Sigismund, for the bell tower
of St Vitus's Cathedral.
During Rudolph II's reign
(1576–1612), the tower
became a laboratory for
alchemists. In 1649, when
the Swedish army occupied
the castle, gunpowder
exploded in the tower,
causing serious damage.
Nevertheless, it was used
as a gunpowder store
until 1754, when it was
converted into flats for
the sacristans of the
cathedral. Today, it houses
a permanent exhibition
on the Castle Guard.

Prague Castle Picture Gallery
Obrazárna Pražského Hradu

📍D3 🏛Prague Castle,
the second courtyard
Ⓜ Malostranská,
Hradčanská 🚌22
🕐9am–5pm daily (Nov–
Mar: to 4pm) 🌐hrad.cz

The gallery was created
in 1965 to hold works of
art collected since the
reign of Rudolph II. Though
most of the collection was
looted by the Swedes in
1648, many interesting
paintings remain. Works
from the 16th to 18th
centuries form the bulk

of the collection, but there are also sculptures, among them a copy of a bust of Rudolph by Adriaen de Vries. The Picture Gallery houses many of Rudolph's best paintings. Highlights include Titian's *The Toilet of a Young Lady*, Rubens' *The Assembly of the Olympic Gods* and Guido Reni's *The Centaur Nessus Abducting Deianeira*. Master Theodoric, Veronese, Tintoretto, and the Czech Baroque artists Jan Kupecký and Petr Brandl are among other artists represented.

St George's Basilica and Convent
Bazilika Sv. Jiří

Q D3 **⌂** Jiřské náměstí
M Malostranská,
Hradčanská **🚋** 22
🕐 9am–5pm daily (Nov–Mar: to 4pm) **W** hrad.cz

Founded by Prince Vratislav (915–21), the basilica is the best-preserved Romanesque church in Prague. In 973, it was enlarged when the adjoining St George's Convent was established

here, and rebuilt following a fire in 1142. The massive twin towers and austere interior have been carefully restored to give a good idea of the church's original appearance. The rusty red façade was a 17th-century Baroque addition.

Buried here is St Ludmila, widow of the 9th-century ruler Prince Bořivoj. She became Bohemia's first female Christian martyr when she was strangled as she knelt at prayer.

Lobkowicz Palace
Lobkovický Palác

Q E3 **⌂** Jiřská 3
M Malostranská
🚋 2, 12, 15, 18, 20, 22
🕐 10am–6pm daily
W lobkowicz.com

Dating from 1570, this is one of the palaces that sprang up after the fire of 1541, when the area was largely destroyed. Some original *sgraffito* on the façade has been preserved, but most of the present palace is Carlo Lurago's 17th-century

reconstruction for the Lobkowicz family, who had inherited it in 1627. The most splendid room is the 17th-century banqueting hall with its mythological frescoes by Fabián Harovník. The palace once formed part of Prague's National Museum, but has since been returned to the Lobkowicz family. It now houses the valuable Princely Collections, an exhibition of paintings, decorative arts, original music scores annotated by Beethoven and Haydn, and musical instruments.

←

The rusty red façade of St George's Basilica

South Gardens

Jiřní Zahrady

Q D3 **A** Prague Castle (access from Old Castle Steps, New Castle Steps or Old Royal Palace) **M** Malostranská **🚊** 2, 12, 15, 18, 20, 22 **Q** Apr-Oct: 10am-6pm daily **W** hrad.cz

The gardens occupy the long narrow band of land below the castle overlooking the Malá Strana. Several small gardens have been linked to form what is now known as the South Gardens. The oldest, the Paradise Garden (Rajská zahrada), laid out in 1562, contains a circular pavilion built for Emperor Matthias in 1617. Its carved wooden ceiling shows the emblems of the 39 countries of the Habsburg Empire. The Garden on the Ramparts (Zahrada Na valech) dates from the 19th century. It occupies a former vegetable patch

and is famous as the site of the defenestration of 1618. Two obelisks were erected by Ferdinand II to mark the spots where they landed. In the former Hartig Garden is a Baroque music pavilion designed by Giovanni Battista Alliprandi. Beside it stand four statues of Classical gods by Antonín Braun.

Belvedere

Belvedér

Q E2 **A** Prague Castle, Royal Garden **M** Malostranská, Hradčanská **🚊** 22 to Královský Letohrádek **Q** 10am-6pm Tue-Sun during exhibitions only

Built by Ferdinand I for his beloved wife Anne, the Belvedere – completed in 1564 – is considered one of the finest Italian Renaissance buildings north of the Alps. Also known as Queen Anne's

Summerhouse (Letohrádek Královny Anny), it is an arcaded building with slender Ionic columns topped by a roof shaped like an inverted ship's hull clad in blue green copper. The main architect was Paolo della Stella, who was also responsible for the ornate reliefs inside.

In the middle of the small geometrical garden in front of the palace stands the Singing Fountain. Dating from 1568, it owes its name to the musical sound the water makes as it hits the bronze bowl. The fountain was cast by Tomáš Jaroš, the famous bell founder, who lived and worked in the Powder Tower.

Many of the Belvedere's works of art were plundered by the Swedish army in 1648. The statues stolen included Dutch artist Adriaen de Vries's 16th-century bronze of *Mercury and Psyche*, now in the

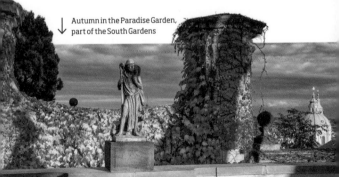

↓ Autumn in the Paradise Garden, part of the South Gardens

Louvre in Paris. Today, the Belvedere is used as an art gallery.

Royal Garden
Královská Zahrada

Q D2 **⌂** Prague Castle, U Prašného mostu **M** Malostranská, Hradčanská **🚋** 22 **🕐** May-Oct: 10am-6pm daily **W** hrad.cz

The Royal Garden was created in 1535 for Ferdinand I. Its appearance has been altered over time, but some examples of 16th-century garden architecture have survived, notably the Belvedere and the Ball Game Hall (Míčovna), built by Bonifaz Wohlmut in 1569. The building is covered in beautiful, though much restored, Renaissance *sgraffito*. The garden is stunning in spring when thousands of tulips bloom.

Riding School
Jízdárna

Q C2 **⌂** Prague Castle **C** 224 372 415 **M** Malostranská, Hradčanská **🚋** 22 **🕐** 10am-6pm during exhibitions

The 17th-century Riding School forms one side of U Prašného mostu, a road that runs to the northern side of Prague Castle via Deer Moat. In the 1920s, it was converted into an exhibition hall, which now holds important art exhibitions. A garden provides excellent views of St Vitus's Cathedral and the northern forti-fications of the castle.

Sternberg Palace
Šternberský Palác

Q C3 **⌂** Hradčanské náměstí 15 **M** Hradčanská, Malostranská **🚋** 22 **🕐** 10am-6pm Tue-Sun **W** ngprague.cz

Franz Josef Sternberg founded the Society of Patriotic Friends of the Arts in Bohemia in 1796. Fellow noblemen would lend their finest pictures and sculpture to the society, which had its headquarters in the early 18th-century Sternberg Palace. Since 1949, the fine Baroque building has been used to house the Prague National Gallery's collection of European art, with its superb range of Old Masters.

The gallery is arranged over three floors that surround the central palace courtyard. The collection focuses on European art from the 15th to the 19th century, and some famous names of the period, such as Tintoretto, Tiepolo, Guardi, El Greco, Goya, Rembrandt Rubens and van Dyck, are all rep-resented here.

EAT & DRINK

Malý Buddha
Bedecked in Tibetan prayer flags and other Buddhist regalia, this unexpected haven of peace serves vegetarian Vietnamese snacks.

Q B4 **⌂** Úvoz 46 **C** 220 513 894 **🕐** Mon

Villa Richter
Located just outside the castle, this stylish place has two eateries: one serving Italian dishes, the other specializing in Czech food and wine.

Q F2 **⌂** Staré zámecké schody 6 **W** villarichter.cz

Ⓚ Ⓚ Ⓚ

U černého vola
Enjoy some Kozel beer in this traditional Czech pub.

Q B4 **⌂** Loretánské náměstí 1 **C** 220 513 481

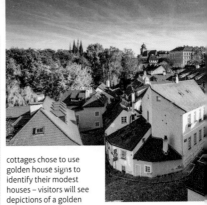

Pohořelec

🔲 B4 🚊 22, 25

First settled in 1375, this is one of the oldest parts of Prague. The name Pohořelec means "place destroyed by fire", a fate the area has suffered three times in the course of its history – the last time being in 1741. It is now a large open square on a hill high over the city and part of the main access route to Prague Castle. In the centre stands a large monument to St John Nepomuk (1752), thought to be by Johann Anton Quitainer. The houses around the square are mainly Baroque and Rococo.

New World

Nový Svět

🔲 B3 🚊 22, 25 to Brusnice

Now a charming street of small cottages, Nový Svět (New World) used to be the name of this area of Hradčany. Developed in the mid-14th century to provide houses for the castle workers, the area was twice destroyed by fire, the last time in 1541. Most of the cottages date from the 17th century. They have been spruced up, but are otherwise unspoilt and very different in character from the rest of Hradčany. In defiance of their poverty, the inhabitants of these cottages chose to use golden house signs to identify their modest houses – visitors will see depictions of a golden pear, a grape, a foot, a bush and an acorn. Plaques identify No 1 as the former home of Rudolph II's brilliant court astronomer, Tycho Brahe, and No 25 as the birthplace of the great Czech violinist and composer František Ondříček.

Černín Palace and Garden

Černínský Palác a Zahrada

🔲 B4 🏛 Loretánské náměstí 5 🚊 22, 25

⏱ Garden: May-Oct: 10am-5pm daily

🌐 mzv.cz

Constructed in 1668 for Count Černín of Chudenice, Imperial Ambassador to Venice, Prague's Černín Palace is arguably the Italian architect Francesco Caratti's masterpiece. It is 150 m (500 ft) long with a row of 30 Corinthian half-columns running the length of its upper storeys.

The building suffered as a result of its position on one of Prague's highest hills. It was looted by the French in 1742 and badly damaged in the Prussian bombardment of the city in 1757. In 1851, the then impoverished Černín family sold the palace to the state and it became a barracks. After Czechoslovakia was created in 1918, the palace was restored to its original design and became the Ministry of Foreign Affairs. It is closed to the public.

The beautiful two-tiered garden, originally designed by Francesco Caratti, features two pools, a cascade fountain and a small pavilion.

↑ Delightful houses and cobbles on winding Nový Svět

Capuchin Monastery

Kapucínský Klášter

📍 B3 🏛 Loretánské náměstí 6 🚊 22, 25 ⛪ To the public except the church

Bohemia's first Capuchin monastery was founded here in 1600. It is connected to the neighbouring Loreta by an overhead roofed passage. Attached to the monastery is the Church of Our Lady Queen of Angels, a single-naved building with plain furnishings, which is typical of the ascetic Capuchin order.

The church is famous for its statue of the Madonna and Child. Emperor Rudolph II liked the statue so much he asked the Capuchins to give it to him for his private chapel. The monks agreed, but the statue made its way back to the church. Rudolph had the Madonna brought back three times, but each time she returned to her original position. The emperor eventually gave up and presented her with a gold crown and a robe.

Martinic Palace

Martinický Palác

📍 C3 🏛 Hradčanské náměstí 8 Ⓜ Malostranská, Hradčanská 🚊 22 🌐 martinickypalac.cz

During restoration of the Martinic Palace in the 1970s, workmen uncovered its original 16th-century façade decorated with ornate cream-and-brown *sgraffito*. The exterior depicts Old Testament scenes, including the story of Joseph and Potiphar's wife. More *sgraffito* in the courtyard shows the story of Samson and the Labours of Hercules.

The palace was enlarged by Jaroslav Bořita of Martinic, who had survived being thrown from a window of the Royal Palace in 1618.

According to an old legend, between 11pm and midnight, the ghost of a fiery black dog appears at the palace and accompanies walkers as far as the Loreta. Visitors can tour the palace (call 603 458 601 to book) or visit a small museum of musical machines.

Schwarzenberg Palace

Schwarzenberský Palác

📍 C4 🏛 Hradčanské náměstí 2 Ⓜ Malostranská, Hradčanská 🚊 22 🕐 10am-6pm Tue-Sun 🌐 ngprague.cz

From a distance, the façade of this grand Renaissance palace appears to be clad in pyramid-shaped stonework. On closer inspection, this turns out to be an illusion created by *sgraffito* patterns incised on a flat wall. Built originally for the Lobkowicz family by the Italian architect Agostino Galli in 1545–76, the gabled palace is Florentine rather than Bohemian in style. It passed through several hands before the Schwarzenbergs, a leading family in the Habsburg Empire, bought it in 1719. Much of the interior decoration has survived, including four painted ceilings on the second floor dating from 1580.

Following renovation, the palace became home to the National Gallery's collection of Baroque art.

A SHORT WALK
PRAGUE CASTLE

Distance 1.5 km (1 mile) **Nearest tram** Pražský hrad
Time 15 minutes

The majestically located and architectually varied Prague Castle complex is a fascinating place for a leisurely walk. Despite periodic fires and invasions, the castle has retained churches, chapels, halls and towers from every period of its history, from the Gothic splendour of St Vitus's Cathedral to the Renaissance additions of Rudolph II. This route through the grounds takes in all the main highlights, but visitors can easily spend a whole day in the complex exploring the interior of the buildings.

Used in the past for storing gunpowder and as a bell foundry, the Powder Tower is now a museum.

The Prague Castle Picture Gallery, housed in the restored stables, displays Renaissance and Baroque paintings.

To Royal Garden

President's office

Second courtyard

Chapel of the Holy Cross

Matthias Gate (1614)

The castle gates are crowned by copies of 18th-century statues of Fighting Giants by Ignaz Platzer.

FINISH

First courtyard

START

Steps down to Malá Strana

Theresian Wing

Several 18th-century statues decorate the South Gardens laid out in the old ramparts.

Did You Know?

The courtyards date from 1753-75 when the whole area was rebuilt in Baroque and Neo-Classical styles.

← Striking interior of Romanesque St George's Basilica

Golden Lane's picturesque artisans' cottages were built along the castle wall in the late 16th century for the castle's guards and gunners.

PRAGUE CASTLE AND HRADČANY

Locator Map

St George's Convent

White Tower

The grim Dalibor Tower is named for a prisoner who played his violin in return for food.

0 metres   60
0 yards   60

N ↑

Exquisite works of art from the Lobkowicz family's private collection are housed in the Lobkowicz Palace.

Inside St George's Basilica is the vaulted chapel of the royal Bohemian martyr St Ludmilla, decorated with 16th-century paintings.

JIŘSKÁ

The uniform exterior of the Old Royal Palace conceals many fine Gothic and Renaissance halls. Coats of arms cover the walls and ceiling of the Room of the New Land Rolls.

→ Historic houses line cobbled Golden Lane

MALÁ STRANA

Crossing the spectacular Charles Bridge from the Old Town to Malá Strana is a truly memorable experience. Many find that the picturesque streets, grand palaces and secret gardens of Malá Strana make it Prague's most attractive quarter. It's a place where you'll need sturdy shoes and strong legs as the streets rise steeply from the river to the castle. Baroque is the dominating architectural style here with some of the city's grandest structures adorning the small squares. Malá Strana has some of Prague's best eating and drinking options.

Malá Strana Bridge Tower and the smaller Judith Bridge Tower ↓

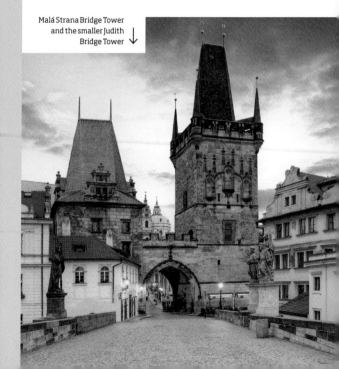

↑ The Small Fürstenberg Garden, with the dome of Gloriette on the lower level and orangeries on the second

PALACE GARDENS
PALÁCOVÉ ZAHRADY

📍 E3 🏠 Valdštejnská 14 Ⓜ Malostranská 🚊 2, 12, 15, 18, 20, 22 🕐 Apr–Oct: 10am–6pm daily (May–Sep: to 7pm) 🅦 palacove-zahrady.cz

Laid out on the steep hillside beneath Prague Castle, the lush Palace Gardens make ingenious use of pavilions, stairways and terraces.

Five beautiful palatial gardens – Ledeburg, Small and Large Pálffy, Kolowrat, and Small Fürstenberg – have been linked together to form one complex. Each has their own distinct layout and provide a peaceful place to escape the bustle of the city. Climb the winding stairways to explore the terraces, with their fragrant plants, Baroque architecture, fountains and pavilions. Concerts and social events are regularly held in the gardens.

HISTORY OF THE GARDENS

The steep slopes below Prague Castle were covered with vineyards and gardens during the Middle Ages. However, in the 16th century, nobles laid out formal terraced gardens based on Italian Renaissance models. Most of these gardens were rebuilt during the 18th century and decorated with Baroque statuary and fountains.

CHARLES BRIDGE

KARLŮV MOST

📍F5 🚋Malá Strana side: 12, 15, 20, 22 to Malostranské náměstí, then walk down Mostecká; Staré Město side: 2, 17, 18 to Karlovy lázně ⏰Malá Strana & Old Town bridge towers: from 10am daily (Mar & Oct: to 8pm; Apr–Sep: to 10pm; Nov–Feb: to 6pm)

The spectacular Charles Bridge, Prague's most familiar monument, has witnessed processions, battles, executions and, increasingly, film shoots since its construction. It is 520 m (1,706 ft) long and is built of sandstone blocks, rumoured to be strengthened by mixing mortar with eggs.

Charles Bridge was commissioned by Charles IV in 1357 to replace the Judith Bridge, which had been destroyed by floods in 1342. Architect Peter Parler built it in Gothic style and it connects the Old Town with the Malá Strana. Until 1841, Charles Bridge was the only crossing over the Vltava. The statues were added from 1683 onwards, but before this the bridge's original decoration was a simple cross.

The Bridge Towers

Charles Bridge has two striking Gothic bridge towers – the Old Town Bridge Tower is one of the finest buildings of its kind. Designed by Peter Parler and built at the end of the 14th century, it was an integral part of the Old Town's fortifications. In 1648, it was badly damaged and the west side still bears the scars. The Old Town tower served as a prison, while the Malá Strana Bridge Tower, built in

the 15th century, was originally used as a storehouse and watchtower. Both towers now house exhibitions exploring the history of the bridge. For great views of the Vltava and the city, head to the viewing gallery of either tower. There is an admission charge for both bridge towers.

Statues

The bridge's most distinguishing feature is its gallery of 30 statues. The religious figures were installed from 1683 onwards to lead people back to the church. The first statue – of St John Nepomuk – was added in 1683, inspired by Bernini's sculptures on Rome's Ponte Sant'Angelo. Some, such as Bohn's Calvary, are politically controversial; others, such as Braun's St Luitgard, are incomparably lovely. Today all the statues are copies, with the originals preserved in the city's museums.

↑ Statue of St Cyril and St Methodius (1938), who were Greek missionaries

↓ Crowds crossing the Old Town side of Charles Bridge

ST JOHN NEPOMUK

The cult of St John Nepomuk, canonized in 1729, was promoted by the Jesuits to rival Jan Hus (p74). Jan Nepomucký, vicar-general of the Archdiocese of Prague, was arrested in 1393 by Wenceslas IV along with others who had displeased him. The king had St John thrown off Charles Bridge, where he drowned. At the base of St John's statue on Charles Bridge is a brass relief showing a man diving into the river. Rubbing it to attract good luck is an old local tradition.

PETŘÍN HILL
VRCH PETŘÍN

⚐ D5 **⌂ Petřín** **🚌 9, 12, 15, 20, 22, then take funicular railway** **Ⓜ 143, 170, 191**

Rising above Malá Strana, wooded Petřín Hill provides some welcome greenery and an escape from the crowds. Stroll along old pathways or take the funicular from Újezd to see the sights atop the hill.

Hunger Wall
Hladová Zeď

⌂ Újezd, Petřín, Strahovská

The great fortifications built around the southern edge of the Malá Strana on the orders of Charles IV in 1360–62 have been known for centuries as the Hunger Wall. Running from Újezd across Petřín Park to Strahov, nearly 1,200 m (1,300 yards) of the wall survive, complete with crenellated battlements and a platform for marksmen on its inner side. The story behind the name is that Charles commissioned its construction with the aim of providing employment to the poor during a period of famine in the 1360s.

Petřín Lookout Tower
Petřínská Rozhledna

🕐 10am-10pm daily (Mar & Oct: to 8pm; Nov-Feb: to 6pm) **🌐 muzeumprahy. cz/prazske-veze**

The most conspicuous landmark in Petřín Park is an imitation of the Eiffel Tower, built for the Jubilee Exhibition of 1891. The octagonally shaped tower

Petřín Hill, with its iconic Lookout Tower

is only 60 m (200 ft), a quarter of the height of the Eiffel Tower. A spiral staircase of 299 steps leads up to the viewing platform. A lift is also available. The views from the top are spectacular with all of Prague's major sights laid out below. On a clear day, you can see as far as Bohemia's highest peak, Sněžka in the Krkonoše (Giant) Mountains, 150 km (100 miles) to the northeast.

Funicular Railway
Lanová Dráha

🚇 Újezd ⏰ 9am–11:30pm daily 🌐 dpp.cz

If you want to save your legs, do as visitors have done since the 1890s and take the funicular railway to the top of the hill and walk down. It was originally built to carry visitors to the 1891 Jubilee Exhibition up to the Lookout Tower at the top of Petřín Hill. The cable car offers outstanding views of the city and the castle. At the halfway station, Nebozízek, there is a restaurant, which is an ideal place to pause and soak up the views. The funicular runs from Újezd every 15 minutes and its ticket is also valid on public transport.

Štefánik's Observatory
Štefánikova Hvězdárna

🚇 Petřín 205 ⏰ Tue–Sun; hours vary, check website for details 🌐 observatory.cz

The observatory is named after the famous Slovak politician, astronomer and co-founder of the Czechoslovak Republic, Milan Rastislav Štefánik. Prague's amateur astronomers have been able to enjoy the facilities here on Petřín Hill since 1930. When the weather is good, visitors can use the observatory's telescopes to view the sun's solar disk and flares, the craters of the moon or unfamiliar distant galaxies. There is an exhibition of old astronomical instruments, and various special events for kids are held on Saturdays and Sundays.

Church of St Lawrence
Kostel Sv. Vavřince

According to legend, this church was founded in the 10th century by the pious Prince Boleslav II and St Adalbert on the site of a pagan shrine, but in the 18th century the church was rebuilt in Baroque style. The ceiling of the sacristy is decorated with a painting illustrating the legend. The church is only open for Mass.

↑ Church of St Lawrence's two onion-domed towers and cupola

CHURCH OF ST NICHOLAS
KOSTEL SV. MIKULÁŠE

📍E4 🏠Malostranské náměstí Ⓜ Malostranská 🚋12, 15, 20, 22 🕐9am-5pm daily (Nov-Mar: to 4pm); Belfry: 10am-6pm daily (Apr-Sep: to 10pm; Mar & Oct: to 8pm) 🌐stnicholas.cz

This Baroque church divides and dominates the two sections of Malostranské Square. Spend at least an hour savouring one of the city's most spectacular buildings.

Building began in 1703, and the last touches were put to the glorious frescoed nave in 1761. This prominent landmark is the acknowledged masterpiece of father-and-son architects Christoph and Kilian Ignaz Dientzenhofer, Prague's greatest exponents of the High Baroque style, although neither lived to see the completion of the magnificent church. The exquisite carvings, statues, frescoes and paintings inside the building are by leading artists of the day, and include a fine Crucifixion of 1646 by Karel Škréta.

Baroque organ

← Panoramic view of the Church of St Nicholas

DIENTZENHOFER FAMILY

Christoph Dientzenhofer (1655-1722) came from a family of Bavarian master builders. His son Kilian Ignaz (1689-1751) was born in Prague and educated at the Jesuit Clementinum. They were responsible for the greatest treasures of Jesuit-influenced Prague Baroque architecture, including several churches and the Břevnov Monastery. The Church of St Nicholas, their last work, was completed by Kilian's son-in-law, Anselmo Lurago.

Entrance from west side of Malo-stranské Square

František Palko's fresco, The Celebration of the Holy Trinity, fills the dome.

Dome

The belfry has a viewing gallery, which offers fabulous city views.

The curving façade has a number of statues, one of which depicts St Paul.

Pulpit

↑ The interior of the church reaches 49 m (161 ft), which makes it the highest in Prague.

Entrance to Belfry

High Altar

Statues of the Church Fathers

Chapel of St Francis Xavier

Chapel of St Catherine

↑ Cross section of the Church of St Nicholas, showing the superb interior

 INSIDER TIP
Concerts

Appreciate the church's Baroque grandeur at a concert of sacred music played on the historic organ. Check the website for upcoming performances.

EXPERIENCE MORE

Wallenstein Palace and Garden

Valdštejnský palác a zahrada

Q E3 **⌂** Valdštejnské náměstí 4 **M** Malostranská **🚋** 2, 12, 15, 18, 20, 22 **Q** Palace: 10am–5pm Sat & Sun; Garden: 10am–6pm daily (Jun–Sep: to 7pm) **w** senat.cz

The first large secular building of the Baroque era in Prague, the palace stands as a monument to the fatal ambition of military commander Albrecht von Wallenstein (1581–1634). His string of victories over the Protestants in the Thirty Years' War made him vital to Emperor Ferdinand II. Though he was already showered with titles, Wallenstein started to covet the crown of Bohemia. When he dared independently to enter into negotiations with the enemy, he was killed on the emperor's orders by a group of mercenaries in the town of Cheb in 1634.

Wallenstein's intention was to overshadow even Prague Castle with his palace, which was built between 1624 and 1630. In order to obtain a suitable site, he had to first purchase and demolish 23 houses, three gardens and the municipal brick kiln. Today, the palace is used as the headquarters of the Czech Senate (the upper house of parliament) and is open to the public. The magnificent main hall rises to a height of two storeys with a ceiling fresco of Wallenstein himself portrayed as Mars, the god of war, riding in a triumphal chariot. The architect, Andrea Spezza, and nearly all of the artists that were employed for the decoration of the palace were Italians.

The beautiful gardens are laid out as they were when Wallenstein dined in the huge *sala terrena* (garden pavilion) that looks out over a fountain and rows of bronze statues. These are copies of works by Adriaen de Vries that were stolen by the Swedes in 1648. There is also a pavilion with fine frescoes showing scenes from the legend of the Argonauts and the Golden Fleece – Wallenstein was a holder of the Order of the Golden Fleece, the highest order of chivalry awarded by the Holy Roman Empire. At the far end of the garden is a large ornamental pond with a central statue. Behind this stands the old Riding School which is now used to house special temporary art exhibitions by the National Gallery. Both the gardens and the riding school have undergone substantial restoration.

Malostranské Square

Malostranské náměstí

Q E4 **M** Malostranská **🚋** 12, 15, 20, 22

The centre of life in the Malá Strana since its foundation in 1257, the square started life as a large marketplace in the outer bailey of Prague Castle. But soon, buildings sprang up in the middle of the square dividing it in half and a gallows and pillory were erected in its lower part. Today, the square is home to a number of restaurants and cafés. Most of the

houses around the square have a medieval core, but all were rebuilt during the Renaissance and Baroque periods. The centre of the square is dominated by the splendid Baroque church of St Nicholas. The large building beside it was a Jesuit college. Along the upper side of the square, facing the church, runs the vast Neo-Classical façade of Lichtenstein Palace. In front of it stands a column raised in honour of the Holy Trinity to mark the end of a plague epidemic in 1713. Other important buildings include the Malá Strana Town Hall with its splendid Renaissance façade, and the Sternberg Palace, built on the site of the outbreak of the fire of 1541, which destroyed most of the Malá Strana.

Beside it stands the Smiřický Palace. Its turrets and hexagonal towers make it an unmistakable landmark on the northern side of the lower square. The Baroque Kaiserstein Palace is situated at the eastern side.

On the façade is a bust of the great Czech soprano Emmy Destinn (Ema Destinnová), who lived there between 1908 and 1914.

The lovely gardens of Wallenstein Palace, with statues

EAT

Nebozízek

One of the city's best park restaurants, Nebozízek offers indoor and outdoor seating and dining with a view. Prices are reasonable for the location.

⚑ **D6** ⌂ **Petřínské sady 411** 🌐 **nebozizek.cz**

U Knoflíčků

This old-school Czech bakery-café sells cakes, sandwiches and coffee at very low prices. Getting a table can be tricky.

⚑ **E6** ⌂ **U Lanové Dráhy 1** ☎ **777 235 139**

Café de Paris

The signature dish at this Swiss-French-style café is beef *entrecôte* in a creamy sauce. Cosy atmosphere and friendly hosts.

⚑ **E5** ⌂ **Velkopřevorské náměstí 4** 🌐 **cafedeparis.cz**

Café Savoy

Dating from 1893, this typically grand old Austrian-era café is good for a coffee and cake stop or a full-on lunch or dinner.

⚑ **E7** ⌂ **Vítězná 5** 🌐 **ambi.cz**

Hergetova cihelna

With some of the best views of Charles Bridge from any Prague eatery, this crisp, well-run restaurant serves international dishes as well as a smattering of local fare.

⚑ **F4** ⌂ **Cihelná 2b** 🌐 **kampagroup.com**

U krále Brabantského

This authentically charred and rough-hewn medieval tavern serves hearty Bohemian dishes and puts on a nightly fire show.

⚑ **D4** ⌂ **Thunovská 15** 🌐 **krcmabrabant.cz**

Church of Our Lady Victorious

Kostel Panny Marie Vítězné

Q E5 **Ⓐ** Karmelitská 9 **🚋** 12, 15, 20, 22 **🕐** 8:30am-7pm daily (to 8pm Sun); Museum of the Prague Infant Jesus: 9:30am-5pm Mon-Sat, 1-6pm Sun **W** pragjesu.info

The first Baroque building in Prague was the Church of the Holy Trinity, built for the German Lutherans by Giovanni Maria Filippi. It was finished in 1613 but after the Battle of the White Mountain in 1620, the Catholic authorities gave the church to the Carmelites, who rebuilt it and renamed it in honour of the victory. The fabric has survived including the portal. Enshrined on a marble altar in the right aisle is a glass case containing the *Holy Infant Jesus of Prague* (better known by its Italian name – *il Bambino di Praga*). This wax effigy has a record of miracle cures and is one of the most revered images in the Catholic world. It was brought from Spain and presented to the Carmelites in 1628 by Polyxena of Lobkowicz. The Museum of the Prague Infant Jesus, located at the back of the church, traces its history. Among the items on display are the various robes that usually adorn the statue. The colours of the robes change with the liturgical calendar: white at Christmas and Easter, purple for Lent, red for Holy Week and green the rest of the year.

Museum Montanelli

Muzeum Montanelli

Q D4 **Ⓐ** Nerudova 13 **Ⓜ** Malostranská **🚋** 12, 15, 20, 22 **🕐** 2-6pm Tue-Sun (from 1pm Sat & Sun) **W** muzeum montanelli.com

The Museum Montanelli (MuMo) is one of a handful of small private museums to be found in Czechia. MuMo's aim is to present imaginative, modern art in a historical setting, while maintaining the DrAK Foundation's permanent collection. Works by both Czech and international artists are shown through

← The Baroque steeple of the Church of Our Lady Victorious

changing exhibitions. The museum hosts an impressive selection of educational programmes for children, including weekend workshops.

Vrtba Garden

Vrtbovská zahrada

📍 D5 🚇 Karmelitská 25 🚊 Malostranská 🚋 12, 15, 20, 22 🕐 Apr–Oct: 10am–6pm daily 🌐 vrtbovska.cz

Behind Vrtba Palace on Petřín Hill lies a beautiful Baroque garden with balustraded terraces. From the highest part of the garden, there are magnificent views of Prague Castle and the

Malá Strana. The Vrtba Garden was laid out by architect František Maximilián Kaňka in about 1720. The statues of Classical gods and stone vases are the work of Austrian Baroque sculptor Matthias Braun and the paintings in the *sala terrena* (garden pavilion) in the lower part of the garden are by Czech Baroque artist Václav Vavřinec Reiner.

Nerudova Street

Nerudova ulice

📍 D4 🚇 Malostranská 🚋 12, 15, 20, 22 🚌 292

A picturesque narrow street leading up to Prague Castle, Nerudova is named after the poet and journalist Jan Neruda, who wrote many short stories set in this part of Prague. He lived in the house called At the Two Suns (No 47)

between 1845 and 1857. Until the introduction of house numbers in 1770, Prague's houses were distinguished by signs. Neruda's houses have a splendid selection of heraldic beasts and emblems. Sightseers making their way up Neruda's steep slope should look out in particular for the Red Eagle (No 6), the Three Fiddles (No 12), the Golden Horseshoe (No 34), the Red Lion (No 41), the Green Lobster (No 43) and the White Swan (No 49).

There are also a number of grand Baroque buildings that line the street, including the Thun-Hohenstein Palace (No 20, now the Italian embassy) and the Morzin Palace (No 5, the Romanian embassy). The latter has a façade with two massive statues of moors (a pun on the name Morzin) supporting a semicircular balcony on the first floor. Another impressive façade is that of the Church of Our Lady of Unceasing Succour, the church of the Theatines, an order founded during the Catholic Counter-Reformation of the 16th and 17th centuries.

← Colourful buildings on Nerudova Street, one of Prague's prettiest streets

Grand Priory Square and the Lennon Wall

Velkopřevorské náměstí

◉ E5 Ⓜ Malostranská
🚋 12, 15, 20, 22

On the northern side of this small leafy square stands the former seat of the Grand Prior of the Knights of Malta. In its present form, the palace dates from the 1720s. The doorways, windows and decorative vases were made at the workshop of Matthias Braun. On the opposite side of the square is the Buquoy Palace, now the French embassy, a Baroque building roughly contemporary with the Grand Prior's Palace.

One of Prague's more unusual sights, the Lennon Wall is a large piece of rolling graffiti on the wall of the Grand Priory, created after The Beatles member John Lennon was murdered in 1980. The location was the focus of anti-Communist protest throughout the 1980s; since those days it has been painted over several times, only for the graffiti to reappear overnight.

At the Three Ostriches

U Tří Pštrosů

◉ E4 🏠 Dražického náměstí 12 📞 777 876 667 Ⓜ Malostranská
🚋 12, 15, 20, 22

Many of Prague's colourful house signs indicated the trade carried on in the premises. In 1597, Jan Fux, an ostrich-feather merchant, bought this house by Charles Bridge. At the time, ostrich plumes were fashionable as decoration for hats among the courtiers and officers at Prague Castle. Fux even supplied feathers to foreign armies. So successful was his business that in 1606 he had the house rebuilt and decorated with a large fresco of ostriches. The building is now a hotel and restaurant.

Maltese Square

Maltézské náměstí

◉ E5 🚋 12, 15, 20, 22

The pretty square takes its name from the Priory of the Knights of Malta, which used to occupy this part of the city. At the northern end stands a group of sculptures featuring St John the Baptist by Ferdinand Brokoff. It is part of a fountain erected in 1715 to mark the end of a plague epidemic.

Most of the buildings surrounding the square were originally Renaissance houses belonging to prosperous townspeople, but in the 17th and 18th centuries, the Malá Strana was taken over by the Catholic nobility and many of the buildings were converted to flamboyant Baroque palaces. The largest, Nostitz Palace, stands on the southern side. It was built in the mid-17th century then, in about 1720, a balustrade was

added with Classical vases and statues of emperors. The palace now houses the Ministry of Culture and, in summer, concerts are held here.

Church of St Thomas
Kostel Sv. Tomáše

◉ E4 **⌂** Josefská 8 **☎** 257 530 556 **Ⓜ** Malostranská **🚊** 12, 15, 20, 22 **◷** 9am–4pm Mon-Sat

Founded by Wenceslas II in 1285 as the monastery church of the Augustinians, the original Gothic church was completed in 1379. In the Hussite period, it was one of the few churches to remain Catholic. As a result, it suffered serious fire damage at the hands of the pre-Protestant Hussite forces. During the reign of Rudolph II, St Thomas's developed strong links with the Imperial court. Several members of Rudolph's entourage were buried here, such as architect Ottavio Aostalli and the sculptor Adriaen de Vries. In 1723, the church was struck by lightning and Kilian Ignaz

Dientzenhofer was asked to rebuild it. The shape of the original church and the Gothic spire were preserved in the Baroque reconstruction. The interior of the dome and the ceiling frescoes in the nave were painted by Václav Vavřinec Reiner. Above the altar are copies of paintings by Rubens – *The Martyrdom of St Thomas* and a picture of St Augustine. The originals are found in the Sternberg Palace.

Church of Our Lady Beneath the Chain
Kostel Panny Marie Pod Řetězem

◉ E5 **⌂** Lázeňská/Velkopřevorské náměstí 4 **☎** 257 530 824 **Ⓜ** Malostranská **🚊** 12, 15, 20, 22 **◷** For concerts and services

This church, the oldest in the Malá Strana, was founded in the 12th century. King Vladislav II presented it to the Knights of St John, the order which later became known as the Knights of Malta. It stood in the centre of the knights' heavily fortified monastery that guarded the approach to the old Judith Bridge. The church's name refers to the chain used to stop boats getting

↑ The high altar in the Church of Our Lady Beneath the Chain

through without paying customs duties. A Gothic presbytery was added in the 13th century, however, a century later, the original Romanesque church was demolished. Although a new portico was built with a pair of massive square towers, work was then abandoned, and the old nave became a courtyard between the towers and the church. This was given a Baroque facelift in 1640 by Carlo Lurago. The painting by Karel Škréta on the high altar shows the Virgin Mary and John the Baptist coming to the aid of the Knights of Malta in the naval victory over the Turks at Lepanto in 1571.

←

John Lennon's eyes peering out from the graffiti-covered Lennon Wall, which people regularly paint over

Kafka Museum
Kafkovo Muzeum

Q F4 **A** Cihelná 2b
M Malostranská
Ä 2, 12, 15, 18, 20, 22
C 10am–6pm daily
W kafkamuseum.cz

This museum houses the exhibition "The City of Franz Kafka and Prague" dedicated to the author Franz Kafka, who was born in Prague in 1883. He wrote visionary works that are considered some of the 20th century's most important, including *The Trial*, *The Castle* and *The Metamorphosis*.

The exhibition has two sections. Existential Space imagines Prague as a mystical space and explores how the city shaped Kafka's life, while Imaginary Topography examines how Kafka turned Prague into a fantastical place in his works, transcending reality.

Vojan Park
Vojanovy sady

Q F4 **A** U lužického semináře 17
M Malostranská
Ä 2, 12, 15, 18, 20, 22
C 8am–5pm daily (summer: to 7pm; Dec & Jan: to 4pm)

A tranquil spot hidden behind high white walls, Vojan Park dates back to the 17th century, when it was the garden of the Convent of Barefooted Carmelites. Two chapels erected by the order have survived among the park's lawns, fruit trees and flower gardens. One is the Chapel of Elijah, who, because of his Old Testament associations with Mount Carmel, is regarded as the founder of the order. His chapel takes the form of a stalagmite and stalactite cave.

The other chapel, dedicated to St Theresa, was built in the 18th century as an expression of gratitude for the convent's preservation during the Prussian siege of Prague in 1757.

Bridge Street
Mostecká Ulice

Q E5 **M** Malostranská
Ä 12, 15, 20, 22

Since the Middle Ages, this street has linked Charles Bridge with the Malostranské Square. Those crossing the bridge from the Old Town can see the doorway of the old customs house built in 1591 in front of the Judith Tower. On the first floor of the tower, there is a 12th-century relief of a king and a kneeling man. Throughout the 13th and 14th centuries, the area

just to the north of the street was home to the Court of the Bishop of Prague. This was destroyed during the Hussite Wars, but one of its Gothic towers is preserved in the courtyard of the house called At the Three Golden Bells. It can be seen from the higher of the two bridge towers. The street has a mixture of Baroque and Renaissance houses. While walking up to Malostranské Square, look out for the house called At the Black Eagle on the left. It has rich sculptural decoration and a splendid Baroque wrought-iron grille. Kaunic Palace, also on the left, was built in the 1770s. Its Rococo façade has striking stucco decoration and sculptures by Ignaz Platzer.

Italian Street

Vlašská Ulice

D4 **Ⓜ Malostranská**
12, 15, 20, 22 **292**

Italian immigrants started to settle here in the 16th century. Many were artists or craftsmen employed to rebuild and redecorate the castle. Those approaching the street from Petřín will see the former Italian

Baroque and Renaissance houses lining busy Bridge Street

EAT & DRINK

Baráčnická rychta

A wood-panelled beer hall within a 1930s building, this bar serves no-nonsense Czech food and beer.

D4 **Tržiště 23**
baracnickarychta.cz

U kocoura

Excellent Pilsner and good food is served at this pub. Try the national dish *vepřo-knedlo-zelo* (pork loin with sauerkraut and dumplings).

E4 **Nerudova 2**
257 530 107

U malého Glena

In addition to a long drinks menu there are burgers, ribs, Tex-Mex and local fare at this

pub-bar. There's a live jazz venue in the basement.

E4 **Karmelitská 23**
malyglen.cz

U hrocha

Near the British Embassy, this very typical Prague pub has great beer, snacks and the same band of locals enjoying them nightly.

D/E4 **Thunovská 10** **257 533 389**

Jo's Bar

This American expat hangout is a great place to mingle with a friendly international crowd. There's also a club.

E4 **Malostranské náměstí 7** **josbar.cz**

Hospital on the left, a Baroque building with an arcaded courtyard. Today, this building maintains its traditional allegiance as the cultural section of the Italian embassy. The grandest building in the street is the former Lobkowicz Palace, now the German embassy, one of the finest Baroque palaces in Prague. Look out too for the pretty stucco sign on the house called At the Three Red Roses, dating from the 18th century.

Czech Museum of Music

České Muzeum Hudby

🌐 E5 🏛 Karmelitská 2
Ⓜ Malostranská 🚋 12, 15, 20, 22 🕐 10am–6pm Wed–Mon 🌐 nm.cz

Housed in the elegant former 17th-century Baroque Church of St Magdalene, the Museum of Music seeks to present its collection of musical instruments not only as specimens of fine craftsmanship and artistry, but also as mediators between man and music.

The museum is run by the National Museum. Exhibits include a look at the diversity of popular 20th-century music as preserved in television, film, sound recordings and photographs. Also examined here is the intricate production of handcrafted instruments, the history of musical notation and the social occasions linked to certain instruments. Earphones offer high-quality sound reproduction of original recordings made on the instruments displayed. The museum's collections can

be accessed via the study room, and there is a listening studio for the library of recordings. Regular concerts are held along with brilliant temporary exhibitions.

Kampa Island

Kampa

🌐 F5 🚋 9, 12, 15, 20, 22

Kampa, an island formed by a branch of the Vltava known as the Devil's Stream (Čertovka), is a delightfully peaceful corner of the Malá Strana. The stream got its name in the 19th century, allegedly after the diabolical temper of a woman who owned a house nearby in Maltese Square. For centuries, the stream was used as a mill-race and, from Kampa, you can see the remains of three old mills. Beyond the Grand Prior's Mill,

SHOP

Artěl

This high-end design shop specializes in striking Czech crystal and exquisitely coloured and cut glass for the home. It also showcases locally produced jewellery, including some carefully chosen antique pieces. There is another branch located at Platnéřská 7.

🌐 F4 🏛 U Lužického Semináře 7
🌐 artelglass.com

Truhlář marionety

Czech puppetry is now part of UNESCO's list of intangible cultural heritage – see what all the fuss is about at this part-handmade puppet shop, part-museum run by the Truhlář family.

🌐 F4 🏛 U lužického semináře 5
🌐 marionety.com

Elima

The intricately patterned, handmade Polish pottery from Bolesławiec sold at this small shop makes for a striking souvenir, even if it is not strictly from the Czech Republic.

🌐 D4 🏛 Jánský vršek 5
🌐 elimashop.cz

the stream disappears under a small bridge below the piers of Charles Bridge. From here, it flows between rows of houses. Predictably, the area has become known as "the Venice of Prague", but instead of gondolas, visitors will only see canoes paddling past.

For most of the Middle Ages, there were only gardens on Kampa. In the 17th century, the island became well-known for its pottery markets. There are some enchanting houses from this period around Na Kampě Square. Most of the land from here to the southern tip of the island is a park, created from several old palace gardens.

The island all but vanished beneath the Vltava during the floods of 2002, which caused widespread devastation to homes, historic buildings and businesses, many of which required restoration.

Sculpture outside the Kampa Museum of Modern Art ↑

Kampa Museum of Modern Art

Muzeum Kampa

F6 U Sovových mlýnů 2 9, 12, 15, 20, 22 10am–6pm daily museum kampa.cz

Housed in the historic Sova mill, the Kampa Museum of Modern Art has an impressive collection of Central European art – mostly 20th century. The museum was founded by the Czech-American couple Jan and Meda Mládek to house their private collection of drawings, paintings and sculptures. Among the artists on display are Czech abstract painter Frantisek Kupka and Czech Cubist sculptor Otto Gutfreund.

Michna Palace (Tyrš House)

Michnův palác (Tyršův Dům)

E6 Újezd 40 257 007 111 12, 15, 20, 22

In about 1580, Ottavio Aostalli built a summer palace for the Kinský family on the site of an old Dominican convent. In 1623, the building was bought by Pavel Michna of Vacínov, a supply officer in the Imperial Army, who had grown rich after the Battle of the White Mountain. He commissioned a Baroque building that he hoped would rival the palace of his late commander, Albrecht von Wallenstein.

In 1767, the palace was sold to the army and over the years it became a crumbling ruin. After 1918, it was bought by Sokol (a physical culture association) and converted into a gym and sports centre with a training ground in the old palace garden and, dating from 1925, the oldest public swimming pool in Prague. The restored palace was renamed Tyrš House in honour of Sokol's founder, Miroslav Tyrš.

A SHORT WALK

MALÁ STRANA

Distance 1.5 km (1 mile) **Nearest metro**
Malostranská **Time** 15 minutes

The Malá Strana, most of whose grand
Baroque palaces now house embassies,
has preserved much of its traditional
character making it the perfect area for a
stroll. The steep, narrow streets and steps
have an air of romantic mystery, and you
will find fascinating buildings adorned
with statues and house signs at every turn.

*At the Three Little Fiddles,
which is now a restaurant,
acquired its house sign
when it was the home of a
family of violin makers in
around 1700.*

*The Museum
Montanelli hosts
international
exhibitions of
modern art.*

*Thun-Hohenstein Palace (1721–6)
has a doorway crowned with two
sculpted eagles by Matthias
Braun. The palace is now the seat
of the Italian embassy.*

*Morzin Palace has a
striking Baroque
façade with a pair
of sculpted moors.*

NERUDOVA

JÁNSKÝ VRŠEK

BŘETISLAVOVA

TRŽIŠTĚ

VLAŠSKÁ

Did You Know?

The area of Malá Strana
became something of
a party town for the
Viennese nobility in
the 18th century.

*Schönborn Palace,
now the American
Embassy, is
decorated with
caryatids from the
17th century.*

← The Baroque interior of the Church of St Thomas, with its lavish altar

MALÁ STRANA

Locator Map

The Baroque Wallenstein Palace was built by an ambitious commander who wanted to eclipse the majesty of Prague Castle.

Czech National Assembly

FINISH

Plague Column

Wallenstein Gardens

A statue of St Augustine by Hieronymus Kohl (1684) decorates the dramatic Baroque façade of the Church of St Thomas.

START

M A L O S T R A N S K É   N A M Ě S T Í

Malá Strana Town Hall

The cupola and bell tower of the Baroque Church of St Nicholas are the best-known landmarks of Malá Strana.

Malostranské Square is divided in half by the buildings which sprang up after its foundation, including the Church of St Nicholas.

| 0 metres | | 100 |
| 0 yards | | 100 |

N

→ The formal flower beds of the Vrtba Garden

A SHORT WALK
MALÁ STRANA RIVERSIDE

Distance 1.5 km (1 mile) **Nearest metro**
Staroměstská **Time** 15 minutes

On either side of Bridge Street (Mostecká Ulice)
lies a delightful half-hidden world of gently
decaying squares, picturesque palaces, churches
and gardens. When you have run the gauntlet of
the trinket-sellers on Charles Bridge, escape to
Kampa Island to enjoy a stroll in its informal park,
the views across the Vltava weir to the Old Town
and the flocks of swans gliding along the river.

*The Church of St Joseph, with
its monumental Dutch-style
façade, dates from the late
17th century. Inside, there is a
painting of The Holy Family
(1702) on the gilded high altar
by Petr Brandl.*

FINISH

*A major thoroughfare for 750 years,
the narrow Bridge Street leads to
Malostranské Square.*

*House at the
White and
Golden Unicorn*

*Two massive towers survive
from when the Church of Our
Lady Beneath the Chain was
a fortified priory.*

*The Grand Prior's Palace is the
former seat of the Knights
of Malta and dates from the
1720s. Its street wall in Grand
Priory Square features
colourful murals and graffiti.*

*The Baroque
Church of Our Lady
Victorious houses the
famous effigy, the Holy
Infant of Prague.*

In Vojan Park – a former monastery garden – quiet shady paths have been laid out under the apple trees.

Locator Map

0 metres   100

0 yards   100

N ↑

At the Three Ostriches, which is now a hotel, has kept the sign of a seller of ostrich plumes.

The approach to the magnificent 14th-century Charles Bridge, with its Baroque statues, passes under an arch below a Gothic tower.

U LUŽICKÉHO SEMINÁŘE

START

Čertovka (the Devil's Stream)

The Grand Priory Mill has had its wheel meticulously restored, though it now turns very slowly in the sluggish water of the Čertovka, the former millrace.

NA KAMPĚ

Kampa Island's park is a popular place for children and provides a welcome break from the hustle and bustle of the city.

↑ A boat travelling along picturesque Čertovka (Devil's Stream)

NOVÉ MĚSTO

Despite the name, the New Town was founded in the 13th century and it possesses some of the capital's finest historical locations. It was this part of the city that witnessed the biggest changes during the 19th century with many old buildings replaced with multi-storey façades in the Art Nouveau style, among others. This is central Prague's biggest and busiest quarter, home to countless hotels, pubs, restaurants, shops and other businesses. It's still the commercial hub, with Wenceslas Square at its heart, and as such is a grittier, more Czech affair than other areas.

The Dancing House, nicknamed "Ginger and Fred"
↓

↑ The richly decorated, pillared hall, with its impressive marble stairway

NATIONAL MUSEUM
NÁRODNÍ MUZEUM

📍 K7 🏛 Václavské náměstí 68 Ⓜ Muzeum 🚊 11, 13
🕙 10am–6pm Tue–Sun Ⓦ nm.cz

Rising majestically at the upper end of Wenceslas Square is the Neo-Renaissance building of the National Museum, a grand, purpose-built affair that even has its own metro station. The entrance fee is worth it, if only to see the grand marble stairway, the Pantheon, and the interior paintings by František Ženíšek, Václav Brožík and Vojtěch Hynais.

The stern edifice, until recently sporting its 1968 bullet holes, was built in the late 1880s to accommodate the growing collection of the National Museum, which was then spread across various locations. Alongside the National Theatre, it is one of the greatest symbols of the Czech National Revival – both buildings are the work of the same architect, Josef Schulz.

The museum has a central pillared hall with a glass-covered courtyard on either side. On the first floor is the Pantheon. The yard on the right houses the fantastic permanent exhibition, which features large sculptures and monuments from the museum's collection.

On the ground floor there are five halls for temporary exhibitions. The left yard has a café, a shop and a children's play-room on the ground floor. The dome's viewing platform has fabulous city views.

NATIONAL THEATRE
NÁRODNÍ DIVADLO

G7 **Národní třída 2** **Národní třída, line B** **2, 9, 17, 18, 22 to Národní divadlo** **Box office: 9am–6pm daily; Auditorium: only during performances** **narodni-divadlo.cz**

This gold-crested theatre has always been an important symbol of the Czech cultural revival. To see the stunning allegorical ceiling frescoes and Vojtěch Hynais's celebrated stage curtain, take in one of the operas performed here.

Work started on the National Theatre in 1868, funded largely by voluntary contributions. The original Neo-Renaissance design was by the Czech architect Josef Zítek. After its destruction by fire in 1881, Josef Schulz was given the job of rebuilding the theatre, and all the best Czech artists of the period contributed towards its spectacular decoration. The western façade is magnificent; the statues are by Antonín Wagner and represent the Arts. During the late 1970s and early 1980s, the theatre was restored and the New Stage was built by architect Karel Prager.

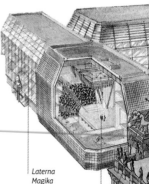

Laterna Magika

The New Stage auditorium

A bronze three-horse chariot

Lobby ceiling

The five arcades of the loggia are decorated with lunette paintings by Josef Tulka, entitled Five Songs.

↑ The grand exterior of the National Theatre

NATIONAL THEATRE FIRE

On 12 August 1881, just days before the official opening, the National Theatre was completely gutted by fire. It was thought to have been started by metalworkers on the roof. Just six weeks later, enough money had been collected to rebuild the theatre. It was finally opened two years later in 1883 with a performance of Czech composer Bedřich Smetana's opera *Libuše*.

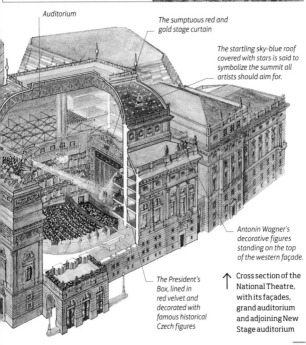

Auditorium

The sumptuous red and gold stage curtain

The startling sky-blue roof covered with stars is said to symbolize the summit all artists should aim for.

Antonín Wagner's decorative figures standing on the top of the western façade.

The President's Box, lined in red velvet and decorated with famous historical Czech figures

↑ Cross section of the National Theatre, with its façades, grand auditorium and adjoining New Stage auditorium

CATHEDRAL OF STS CYRIL AND METHODIUS

KATEDRÁLA SV. CYRILA A METODĚJE

📍H9 🏛Resslova 9 Ⓜ Karlovo náměstí 🚋2, 3, 6, 10, 14, 16, 18, 22, 24
🕐8–9:30am Sat, 9am–noon Sun; Museum and crypt: 9am–5pm Tue–Sun
🌐pravoslavna-katedrala.info

A short walk along busy Resslova Street from Charles Square stands this cathedral, the main church belonging to the Czechoslovak Orthodox congregation. It was here that the final act of a heroic piece of World War II resistance was played out.

This Baroque church, with a pilastered façade and a small central tower, was built in the 1730s. It was dedicated to St Charles Borromeo and served as the church of a community of retired priests, but was closed in 1783. In the 1930s, the church was given to the Czechoslovak Orthodox Church and rededicated to St Cyril and St Methodius, the 9th-century "Apostles to the Slavs".

The Heydrich Terror (heydrichiáda)

In May 1942, seven parachutists who assassinated Reinhard Heydrich, the Nazi governor of Czechoslovakia, hid in the crypt along with members of the Czech Resistance. Surrounded by German troops, they took their own lives on 18 June 1942 rather than surrender. Bullet holes made by German machine guns during the siege can still be seen below the memorial plaque on the outer wall of the crypt. The Nazis were quick to exact revenge for the assassination and judged that the village of Lidice, lying to the west of Prague, was somehow implicated, so they razed it to the ground.

> 💬 **INSIDER TIP**
> **18 June**
>
> Since 1945, every year on 18 June the Cathedral of Sts Cyril and Methodius holds a special service to remember the victims of the Heydrich Terror.

→

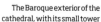

The Baroque exterior of the cathedral, with its small tower

THE CRYPT

Before entering the crypt, there is a small museum that tells the story of the events of 27 May to 18 June 1942. On display are artifacts relating to Nazi rule and the assassination of Heydrich. In the crypt is the memorial to the parachutists, known as the National Monument to the Heroes of the Heydrich Terror. A bronze plaque has been hung on the wall in their memory. The parachutists' last attempts to dig an escape tunnel can also be seen.

↑ Statues of the parachutists line the crypt and on the wall *(left)* is a bronze memorial plaque commemorating these heroes

EXPERIENCE MORE

Wenceslas Square

Václavské náměstí

Q K7 **M** Můstek, Muzeum
🚋 3, 5, 6, 9, 14, 24

Measuring 750 m (825 yd) in length but just 60 m (65 yd) across at the widest point, Prague's main square is more of a gently sloping avenue than a grand piazza. However, it is the epicentre of the city, lined with hotels, restaurants, clubs and shops.

Formally a medieval horse market, the square began to be redeveloped in the 19th century and rapidly become the commercial hub of the city. In 1848 it was renamed Wenceslas Square in honour of Bohemia's patron saint. The majority of the buildings seen today date from the early 20th century and have beautiful Art Nouveau façades.

The square has often been, and continues to be, the scene of numerous marches, political protests and celebrations. It was here that large crowds gathered to celebrate the end of Communism in 1989.

At the top of the square is the National Museum, in front of which stands Josef Myslbek's 1912 equestrian statue of St Wenceslas. The area "under the tail" is a traditional meeting place for locals.

HIDDEN GEM
Králíček Lamp

Near the bottom end of Wenceslas Square, behind the Baťa store, stands the world's only Cubist street lamp, designed by architect Emil Králíček in 1913.

Grand Hotel Europa

Grand Hotel Evropa

Q K6 **M** Václavské náměstí 25 **M** Můstek
🚋 3, 5, 6, 9, 14, 24

Currently in the midst of a renovation project, the Grand Hotel Europa is a wonderfully preserved reminder of the golden age of hotels. It was built in highly decorated Art Nouveau style between 1903 and 1906. Not only has its splendid façade crowned with gilded nymphs survived, but many of the interiors have remained virtually intact, including the original bars, panelling and light fittings.

Church of Our Lady of the Snows

Kostel Panny Marie Sněžné

Q J6 **M** Jungmannovo náměstí 18 **M** Můstek
🕑 9am–6pm daily
W pms.ofm.cz

Charles IV founded this church to mark his coronation in 1347. The church's name refers to a 4th-century miracle in Rome, when the Virgin Mary appeared to the Pope in a dream telling him to build a church to her on the spot where

snow fell in August. Charles's church was never completed, and the building we see today was just the presbytery of the projected church. Over 33 m (110 ft) high, it was finished in 1397, and was originally part of a Carmelite monastery.

The church suffered damage in the Hussite wars and, for a long time, the church was left to decay. In 1603, Franciscans restored the building. The ceiling's intricate net vaulting dates from this period, the original roof having collapsed. Most of the interior decoration, apart from the 1450s pewter font, is Baroque. The monumental three-tiered altar is crowded with statues of saints, and is crowned with a crucifix.

↑ Spring flowers in bloom in the Franciscan Garden

Lucerna Palace and Passage

Palác a pasáž Lucerna

🔘 K7 🚇 Štěpánská 61
🚊 Můstek 🚋 3, 5, 6, 9, 14, 24 ⏰ See website
🌐 lucerna.cz

One of Prague's most engaging modern palaces, Lucerna was built between 1907

and 1920 in the Art Nouveau style by entrepreneur Vácslav Havel. Havel's grandson, Václav, became the first President of the Czech Republic in 1993.

The palace is home to the oldest permanent cinema in Bohemia, dating from 1907. A major centre of Prague film life, the cinema screens award-winning films from festivals around the world. The palace also hosts a variety of concerts and balls in its Great Hall, and contemporary art exhibitions in its gallery.

Franciscan Garden

Františkánská zahrada

🔘 J6 🚇 Můstek ⏰ Apr-Oct: 7am-10pm (Oct: to 8pm); Nov-Mar: 8am-7pm

Originally the garden of a Franciscan monastery, the area opened to the public in 1950 as a tranquil oasis close to Wenceslas Square. Next to the entrance is a Gothic portal leading down to a cellar restaurant called U Františkánů (At the Franciscans). In the 1980s, several of the beds were replanted with herbs, cultivated by the Franciscans in the 17th century. Today, it is a popular spot.

← Grand Hotel Europa's splendid yellow Art Nouveau façade

State Opera
Státní Opera

📍 L7 🏛 Wilsonova 4/
Legerova 75 🚇 Muzeum
🚊 3, 5, 6, 9, 14, 24
🕐 For performances only
🌐 narodni-divadlo.cz

The first theatre built here,
the New Town Theatre,
was pulled down in 1885
to make way for the present
building. This was originally
known as the New German
Theatre, built to rival the
National Theatre.

A Neo-Classical frieze
decorates the pediment
above the columned loggia
at the front of the theatre.
The figures include Dionysus
and Thalia, the muse of
comedy. The interior is
stuccoed, and original
paintings in the auditorium and on the curtain
have been preserved.

In 1945, the theatre
became the city's main
opera house.

Mucha Museum
Muchovo Muzeum

📍 K5 🏛 Panská 7
🚇 Můstek, Náměstí
Republiky 🚊 3, 5, 6, 9,
14, 24 🕐 10am–6pm
daily 🌐 mucha.cz

The 18th-century Kaunicky
Palace is home to the only
museum in the country
dedicated entirely to
the Czech master of Art
Nouveau, Alfons Mucha.
It contains a selection of
more than 100 exhibits,
including paintings and
drawings, sculptures, photographs and personal
memorabilia, though
there are very few of his
most famous works on
show. The central courtyard becomes a terrace
for the café in the summer.

The museum is run by
the Mucha Foundation,
which organizes exhibitions around the world
and works to preserve
Mucha's legacy.

Dancing House
Tančící dům

📍 G9 🏛 Rašínovo nábřeží
80 / Jiráskovo náměstí
🚇 Karlovo náměstí 🚊 5,
17 🕐 Daily

This extraordinary
building is affectionately
known as the "Dancing
House", or "Ginger and
Fred", due to the fact
that its silhouette brings
to mind the famous
American dancing pair,
Fred Astaire and Ginger
Rogers. Built between

1992 and 1996 by Californian architect Frank Gehry and his associate Vlado Milunič, this iconic glass and concrete structure is in fact, two buildings with different façades and of different heights. Most of the building is now a hotel owned by former Czech international football player, Vladimír Šmicer.

For superb panoramic views of the city, visit the restaurant, Céleste, on the top floor.

Church of St Ignatius

Kostel Sv. Ignáce

📍 H9 📍 Ječná 2
📞 221 990 200
Ⓜ Karlovo náměstí
🚊 2, 3, 6, 10, 14, 16, 18, 22, 24 🕐 6am–noon & 3:30–6:30pm daily

With its wealth of gilding and flamboyant stucco decoration, St Ignatius is typical of the Baroque churches built by the Jesuits to impress people with the glamour of their faith. The architects – Italian Carlo Lurago, who started work on the church in 1665, and

Traditional ball in one of the capital's top opera venues, the State Opera

EAT & DRINK

Dynamo

This post-modern diner serves dishes such as rump steak in marinade with thyme and oregano. There is also a wide selection of excellent vegetarian options.

📍 G7 📍 PŠtrossova 29
🌐 dynamorestaurace.cz

U Šumavy

High-ceilinged and old-fashioned, this authentic pub-restaurant is a little piece of the Czech countryside in central Prague. The food is traditional – everything is served with dumplings.

📍 J9 📍 Štěpánská 3
🌐 usumavy.cz

Novoměstský pivovar

This microbrewery serves vast quantities of its own ales as well as platters of Czech food in its twelve sprawling underground beer halls.

📍 J7 📍 Vodičkova 20
🌐 npivovar.cz

Pivovarský dům

Another microbrewery pub serving eight types of beer and Czech pub food. The wood-panelled dining room is particularly popular at lunchtime.

📍 J9 📍 Ječná 16
🌐 pivovarsky dum.com

Czech Paul Ignaz Bayer, who added the tower in 1699 – were also responsible for the adjoining Jesuit College.

The painting on the high altar of The Glory of St Ignatius (St Ignatius Loyola was the founder

of the Jesuit order) is by Jan Jiří Heinsch.

The Jesuits continued to embellish the church's interior right up until the suppression of their order in 1773, adding stucco work and statues of Jesuit and Czech saints.

Charles Square

Karlovo náměstí

📍 H8 Ⓜ Karlovo náměstí
🚋 2, 3, 6, 10, 14, 16, 18, 22, 24

Since the mid-19th century, Prague's largest square has been a park. Though it is surrounded by busy roads, it is still a pleasant – but somewhat shabby – place to sit and read or watch people walking their dogs.

The square began life as a vast cattle market, when Charles IV founded the New Town in 1348. Other goods sold in the square included firewood, coal and pickled herring from barrels. In the centre of the market, Charles had a wooden tower built, where the Imperial crown jewels were put on display once a year.

Church of St Catherine

Kostel Sv. Kateřiny

📍 J9 🏠 Kateřinská 30
🚋 4, 6, 10, 16, 22
⊙ Only for services

St Catherine's stands in the garden of a former convent, founded in 1354 by Charles IV to commemorate his victory at the Battle of San Felice in Italy in 1332. In 1420, during the Hussite revolution, the convent was demolished, but in the 16th century, it was re-built by the Augustinians.

The monastery closed in 1784 and since 1822 it has been used as a military education institute. In 1737, a new Baroque church was built by Bohemian architect Kilian Ignáz Dientzenhofer, but the slender steeple of the old Gothic church was retained. Its octagonal shape has gained it the nickname of "the Prague minaret".

Slavonic Monastery Emauzy

Klášter Na Slovanech-Emauzy

📍 H10 🏠 Vyšehradská 49 🚋 2, 3, 10, 14, 16, 18, 24 ⊙ 11am–5pm Mon–Fri (summer: also Sat; Nov–Mar: to 2pm) 🌐 emauzy.cz

This monastery and church complex are famous in the Czech Republic for having been partially destroyed in an American air raid in 1945. During their reconstruction, the church was given a pair of modern

The statue of writer Eliška Krásnohorská in Charles Square ↓

reinforced concrete spires, instantly recognizable on the Prague skyline. The monastery was founded in 1347 for the Croatian Benedictines, whose services were held in the Old Slavonic language, hence its name "Na Slovanech". In the course of Prague's tumultuous religious history, it has since changed hands many times. In 1446, a Hussite order was formed here, then in 1635, the mona-stery was acquired by Spanish Benedictines. In the 18th century, the complex was given a thorough Baroque treatment, but in 1880 it was taken over by some German Benedictines, who rebuilt almost everything in Pseudo-Gothic (Beuron) style. The monastery has managed to preserve some historically important 14th-century wall paintings, though many were damaged in World War II.

↑ The dynamic façade of the Church of St John of Nepomuk on the Rock

Church of St John of Nepomuk on the Rock

Kostel Sv. Jana Nepomuckého Na Skalce

📍 H10 🚇 Vyšehradská 49 📞 732 601 378
🚊 3, 4, 10, 16, 18, 22, 24
🕐 For services only

One of Prague's smaller Baroque churches, St John of Nepomuk on the Rock is one of Kilian Ignaz Dientzenhofer's most daring designs. Its twin square towers are set at a sharp angle to the church's narrow façade and the interior is based on an octagonal floorplan around a single aisle. The church was completed in 1738, but the double staircase leading up to the west front was not added until the 1770s. On the high altar, there is a wooden model version of Jan Brokof's statue of St John Nepomuk that stands on the Charles Bridge.

Did You Know?

Emperor Charles IV (1346-78) has an asteroid named after him: 16951 Carolus Quartus.

Dvořák Museum
Muzeum Antonína Dvořáka

K9 ☐ Ke Karlovu 20
Ⓜ IP Pavlova 🚊 4, 6, 10, 16, 22 🚌 148 ⏰ 10am–1:30pm & 2–5pm Tue–Sun and for concerts 🌐 nm.cz

One of the most enchanting secular buildings of Prague's Baroque era now houses a museum devoted to the 19th-century Czech composer. On display in the Dvořák Museum are scores and early editions of Antonín Dvořák's works, plus photos and memorabilia, including his piano and viola.

The building was designed by the great Baroque architect Kilian Ignaz Dientzenhofer. Just two storeys high with an elegant tiered mansard roof and salmon-pink walls, the house was completed in 1720 for the Michnas of Vacínov and was originally known as the Michna Summer Palace. It later became known as Villa Amerika, after a nearby inn called Amerika. Between the two pavilions flanking the house is a fine iron gateway, a replica of the Baroque original. In the 19th century, the villa and garden fell into decay. The garden statues and vases, from the workshop of Matthias Braun, date from about 1735. They are

original but heavily restored, as is the interior. The ceiling and walls of the large room on the first floor are decorated with 18th-century frescoes by Austrian painter Jan Ferdinand Schor.

Church of St Stephen
Kostel Sv. Štěpána

J9 ☐ Štěpánská 📞 221 990 200 🚊 4, 6, 10, 16, 22 ⏰ Only for services

Founded by Charles IV in 1351 as the parish church of the upper New Town, St Stephen's was finished in 1401 with the completion of the multi-spired steeple. In the

late 1600s, the Branberg Chapel was added on to the north side of the church. It contains the tomb of the prolific Baroque sculptor Matthias Braun. Most of the subsequent Baroque additions were removed when the church was scrupulously re-Gothicized in the 1870s by Josef Mocker. There are several fine Baroque paintings still here, however, including *The Baptism of Christ* by Karel Škréta at the end of the left-hand aisle and a picture of St John Nepomuk by Jan Jiří Heinsch to the left of the 15th-century pulpit. The church's greatest

←

Antonín Dvořák's piano in the museum and the Dvořák Museum's pink façade *(inset)*

sculptures still decorate the façade and in front of the church stands a group of statues featuring St John Nepomuk (1747) by Ignaz Platzer the Elder. The light and airy interior has a frescoed and stuccoed ceiling, and on the various altars there are lively Baroque paintings. The main altar has one featuring St Ursula.

The adjoining convent has been returned to the Ursuline order and is now a Catholic school. The building to the right is the entrance to the Institute of Endocrinology.

treasure is undoubtedly a Gothic panel painting of the Madonna, known as *Our Lady of St Stephen's,* dating from 1472.

Church of St Ursula
Kostel Sv. Voršily

📍 G7 🚇 Národní 8
🚇 Národní třída 🚊 2, 9, 18, 22

The white and pink Baroque Church of St Ursula was built as part of an Ursuline convent founded in 1672. The original

New Town Hall
Novoměstská radnice

📍 H8 🚇 Karlovo náměstí 23 🚇 Karlovo náměstí 🚊 2, 3, 6, 10, 14, 16, 18, 22, 24 🕐 Tower: Apr–Nov: 10am–6pm Tue–Sun 🌐 nrpraha.cz

The town hall already existed in the 1300s; the Gothic tower was added in the mid-15th century and contains an 18th-century chapel. In the 16th century, it acquired an arcaded courtyard. After the joining-up of

the four towns of Prague in 1784, the town hall ceased to be the seat of the municipal administration and became a courthouse and a prison. It is now used for cultural and social events.

In 1960, a statue of Hussite preacher Jan Želivský was unveiled in front of the New Town Hall. It commemorates the first and bloodiest of many defenestrations. On 30 July 1419, Želivský led a crowd of demonstrators to the town hall to demand the release of some prisoners. When they were refused, they stormed the building and threw the Catholic councillors out of the windows. Those who survived were finished off with pikes.

A SHORT WALK
WENCESLAS SQUARE

Distance 1.5 km (1 mile) **Nearest metro**
Můstek **Time** 15 minutes

Hotels and restaurants occupy many of the buildings around Wenceslas Square, though it remains an important commercial centre. As you walk along, look up at the buildings, most of which date from the turn of the 19th and 20th centuries when the square was redeveloped. There are fine examples of the decorative styles used by Czech architects of the period. Many blocks have covered arcades leading to shops, clubs, theatres and cinemas.

Koruna Palace (1914) is an ornate block of shops and offices. Its corner turret is topped with a crown (koruna).

START

NA PŘÍKOPĚ

🚇 Můstek

U Pinkasů beer hall

Jungmann Square is named after Josef Jungmann (1773–1847), an influential scholar of language and lexicographer, and there is a statue of him in the middle.

Můstek 🚇

The towering Gothic Church of Our Lady of the Snows is only part of a vast church planned during the 14th century.

VODIČKO

Lucerna Palace

Franciscan Garden, a former monastery garden, has been laid out as a small park with a fountain, rosebeds, trellises and a children's playground.

Wiehl House, named fter its architect Antonín Wiehl, was completed in 1896. The five-storey building is in striking Neo-Renaissance style, with a loggia and colourful sgraffito. Mikuláš Aleš designed some of the Art Nouveau figures.

↑ Franciscan Garden and Church of Our Lady of the Snows

← Statues of illustrious Czech scientists and cultural figures in the National Museum's Pantheon

NOVÉ MĚSTO

Locator Map

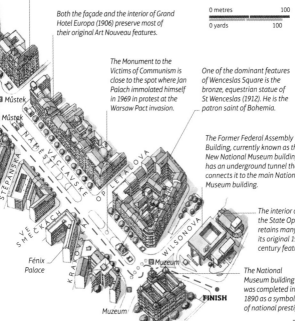

The Assicurazioni Generali Building was where Franz Kafka worked as an insurance clerk for 10 months in 1906–7.

Both the façade and the interior of Grand Hotel Europa (1906) preserve most of their original Art Nouveau features.

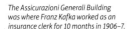

0 metres 100
0 yards 100

N ↑

The Monument to the Victims of Communism is close to the spot where Jan Palach immolated himself in 1969 in protest at the Warsaw Pact invasion.

One of the dominant features of Wenceslas Square is the bronze, equestrian statue of St Wenceslas (1912). He is the patron saint of Bohemia.

The Former Federal Assembly Building, currently known as the New National Museum building, has an underground tunnel that connects it to the main National Museum building.

The interior of the State Opera retains many of its original 19th-century features.

The National Museum building was completed in 1890 as a symbol of national prestige.

Můstek

Můstek

ŠTĚPÁNSKÁ

NÁMĚSTÍ VÁCLAVSKÉ

OPLETALOVA

WILSONOVA

V E SMEČKÁCH

Fénix Palace

KRAKOVSKÁ

Muzeum

FINISH

Muzeum

DAYS OUT FROM PRAGUE

The sights that attract most visitors away from the city are Bohemia's picturesque medieval castles. Karlštejn, with its turrets and towers and immaculate interiors, is one of the most-visited places in the country. Other, less-visited, castles, such as Křivoklát and Konopiště, offer quieter opportunities for exploration. The town of Kutná Hora, with its atmospheric old centre and Gothic Cathedral of St Barbara, is also hugely popular. Other towns worth visiting are the famous spa resorts of Karlovy Vary and Mariánské Lázně.

Konopiště Castle in winter ↓

Tiny St Catherine's Chapel, richly decorated with splendid paintings and semi-precious stones ↓

Karlštejn Castle rises from the forests of Central Bohemia in dramatic Gothic style ↑

KARLŠTEJN CASTLE

25 km (16 miles) SW of Prague 🚆 From Smíchov or Hlavní nádraží to Karlštejn (1.5 km/1 mile from castle; the uphill walk takes around 40 minutes) 🕐 Feb: Sat & Sun, Mar–Dec: Tue–Sun (Jul & Aug: daily); Chapel of the Holy Rood: May–Oct: Tue–Sun (Jul & Aug: daily) 🌐 hrad-karlstejn.cz

Karlštejn Castle, with its turrets, towers and immaculate interiors, is one of the most-visited historic sites in the Czech Republic.

Once a purely 14th-century fortress, built by Charles IV to house the imperial crown jewels, the castle was given a Neo-Gothic makeover in the late 19th century by Czech architect Josef Mocker. It was then that the castle got its ridge roofs, a typical feature of medieval architecture.

Access to the building is by guided tour only. The one-hour-long basic tour leads you through the historic interiors of the first and second floors of the Imperial Palace and visits the treasury. The 100-minute special tour takes in the Chapel of the Holy Cross, one of the most ornate and precious chapels in the Czech Lands. Numbers are limited on this tour, so book well ahead.

A PLACE FOR THE CROWN JEWELS

When Charles IV became Holy Roman Emperor in the mid 1340s, he needed a place to keep the imperial crown jewels as well as his impressive collection of saintly relics. Though the main construction work on the new Karlštejn Castle was carried out by an unknown architect, it's said the emperor personally oversaw the decoration of the interiors. The crown jewels were kept in the Chapel of the Holy Cross until 1420 when the Hussite Wars began. They are now stored in St Vitus's Cathedral.

KUTNÁ HORA

70 km (45 miles) E of Prague From Hlavní nádraží to Kutná Hora, then bus 1 to Kutná Hora-Město From Florenc Palackého náměstí 377 (Tel: 327 515 556) kutnahora.cz

This small town began as a mining community in the late 13th century. Rich deposits of silver were discovered here and soon the town grew into the second most important in Bohemia after Prague. During the 14th century, the Prague *groschen*, minted in Kutná Hora from the local silver, became the most widespread coin in Europe. The town's wealth paid for a number of grand buildings including the Cathedral of St Barbara.

Hrádek - Czech Museum of Silver and Medieval Silver Mine

Hrádek - České muzeum stříbra a středověký stříbrný důl

 Barborská 28 Tue-Sun; check website for details cms-kh.cz

The Hrádek building, originally a fort, is home to the town's silver mining museum. The museum offers two guided tours – the first explores the geology of the region and the development of Kutná Hora following the discovery of silver; the second includes a tour of a 250-m (820-ft) medieval mine and explains how the ore was processed and then minted into coins.

Sedlec Ossuary

Sedlec Kostnice

 Zámecká Hours vary, check website ossuary.eu

One of the creepiest spectacles in the Czech Republic must be the Ossuary of the Church of All Saints in the suburb of Sedlec. The chapel decor was created by

Delightful Kutná Hora, with a mix of different architectural styles

local woodcarver František Rint using the bones of 40,000 people. The bones come from the adjacent cemetery which was downsized in the 15th century, the exhumed bones stacked up against the chapel wall. The finest piece is the chandelier made using one of every single bone in the human body.

Cathedral of St Barbara
Chrám svaté Barbory

🅐 Barborská 🅞 Jan & Feb: 10am-4pm daily; Mar, Nov & Dec: 10am-5pm daily; Apr-Oct: 9am-6pm daily

To the southwest of Kutná Hora stands the Cathedral of St Barbara, with its three massive and tent-shaped spires rising above a forest of flying buttresses. Dedicated to the patron saint of miners, the cathedral is one of Europe's most spectacular Gothic churches. Both the interior and the exterior are richly ornamented, and the huge windows ensure it is filled with light. Many

of the side chapels are decorated with interesting frescoes, some of which depict miners at work and men striking coins in the mint, reflecting the sources of the town's wealth.

Stone House
Kamenný dům

🅐 Václavské náměstí 183 🅞 Tue-Sun; check website for details 🅦 cms-kh.cz

This house, with its richly decorated stone gable, is an important example of European late Gothic architecture. It is now managed by the Czech Museum of Silver and is a testament to how people lived. On display in the house is an exhibition exploring the lives of townspeople between the 17th and 19th centuries. There is also a collection of Gothic sculptures and architectural elements from Kutná Hora in the two-floor cellar.

Italian Court
Vlašský dvůr

🅐 Havlíčkovo náměstí 552 🅞 Daily 🅦 vlassky-dvur.cz

The Italian Court, the former Royal Mint, got its name from the Florentine experts who were employed to set

up the mint and who began stamping the Prague *groschen* here in 1300. Strongly fortified, it was also the royal residence in the town. In the late 14th century, Wenceslas IV commissioned a grand palace to be added. The silver began to run out in the 16th century and the mint closed in 1727. The Italian Court later became the town hall.

There are guided tours of both the Royal Mint and the palace, plus an exhibition on coins and minting in the treasury rooms.

EAT

Pivnice Dačický
A large, traditional beer hall-style restaurant with folksy decor, good draught beer and frequent live music. The menu focuses on Austrian and Czech classics, such as wild boar goulash and Moravian smoked pork.

🅐 Rakova 8 🅦 dacicky.com

EXPERIENCE MORE

Konopiště Castle

🏛 40 km (25 miles) SF of Prague 🚉 From Hlavní nádraží to Benešov, then local bus ⏰ Apr–Nov: 10am–noon & 1–4pm Tue–Sun (Jun–Aug: to 5pm; Oct & Nov: to 3pm) 🌐 zamek-konopiste.cz

Though it originally dates back to the 13th century, this moated castle is essentially a late 19th-century creation. In between, Konopiště had been rebuilt by Baroque architect František Kaňka and in front of the bridge across the moat is a gate (1725) by Kaňka and sculptor Matthias Braun.

In 1887, Konopiště was bought by Archduke Franz Ferdinand, who later became heir to the Austrian throne. It was his assassination in 1914 in Sarajevo that triggered World War I. To escape the Habsburg court's disapproval of his wife, he spent much of his time at Konopiště and amassed arms, armour and Meissen porcelain, all on display in the fine furnished interiors. However, the abiding memory of the castle is of the stags' heads lining the walls.

Veltrusy Château

Veltruský Zámek

🏛 20 km (12 miles) N of Prague 🚉 From Masarykovo nádraží to Kralupy nad Vltavou, then bus ⏰ Feb–Apr & Oct–Dec: Sat & Sun; May–Sep Tue–Sun; Park: dawn to nightfall daily 🌐 zamek-veltrusy.cz

Veltrusy is a small town beside the Vltava, famous for the 18th-century château built by the aristocratic Chotek family. The building is in the shape of a cross, with a central dome and a stair-case adorned with statues representing the months and the seasons. The estate was laid out as an English-style landscaped deer park, covering an area of 300 hectares (750 acres). Near the entrance, there is still an enclosure with a herd of deer.

The Doric and Maria Theresa pavilions, the orangery and the grotto date from the late 18th century. Some 100 different kinds of tree are planted in the park.

Across the river, and accessible from Veltrusy by bus or train, is Nelahozeves Château. This Renaissance castle has an exhibition entitled "Private Spaces: A Noble Family At Home", depicting the life of the Lobkowicz family over five

centuries. Some 12 rooms have been fitted out with period furnishings. On display in the library are the family's art treasures are housed in Lobkowicz Palace.

Every year, Nelahozeves Château hosts a popular classical music festival called Dvořákova Nelahozeves.

↑ The Great Tower emerges above Křivoklát Castle

Křivoklát Castle

🏰 45 km (28 miles) W of Prague 🚂 From Hlavní nádraží via Beroun or from Masarykovo nádraží via Rakovník (1 km/0.6 miles) from castle) 🕐 Times vary, see website 🌐 hrad-krivoklat.cz

This castle, like Karlštejn, owes its appearance to the restoration work of Josef Mocker. It was originally a hunting lodge belonging to early Přemyslid princes and the seat of the royal master

← A pond in the landscaped gardens of Veltrusy Château

of hounds. In the 13th century, King Wenceslas I built a stone castle here, which remained in the hands of Bohemia's kings and the Habsburg emperors until the 17th century.

Charles IV spent some of his childhood here and returned from France in 1334 with his first wife Blanche de Valois. Their daughter Margaret was born in the castle. To amuse his queen and young princess, Charles ordered the local villagers to trap nightingales and set them free in a wooded area just below the castle. Today, visitors can still walk along

the "Nightingale Path". The royal palace is on the eastern side of the triangular castle. This corner is dominated by the Great Tower, at 42 m (130 ft) high. Some of the 13th-century stonework is still visible, but most of the palace dates from the reign of Vladislav Jagiello. On the first floor there is a vaulted Gothic hall, similar to the Vladislav Hall in the Old Royal Palace at Prague Castle. It has an oriel window and a beautiful loggia, and the chapel has a finely carved Gothic altar.

Below the chapel, the Augusta Prison is named for Bishop Jan Augusta of the Bohemian Brethren, imprisoned here in the mid-16th century. The dungeon houses an assortment of torture instruments.

Karlovy Vary

🏠 140 km (85 miles) W of
Prague 🚆 From Hlavní
nádraží 🚌 From Florenc
ℹ️ Lázeňská 14 (355 321
176) 🌐 karlovyvary.cz

Named after Charles IV,
the most visited spa town
in Prague was founded in
1370. Legend has it that
Charles discovered one
of the sources of mineral
water that would make the
town's fortune when one
of his stag hounds fell into
a hot spring. In 1522, a
medical description of
the springs was published,
and by the end of the 16th
century, over 200 spa
buildings had been built
there. Today, there are
12 hot mineral springs –
vary means hot springs in
Czech. The best-known is
the Vřídlo, which rises to
a height of 12 m (40 ft).
At 72°C, it is also the
hottest. The water is said
to be good for digestive
disorders, but it is not
necessary to drink it; the
beneficial minerals can be
taken in the form of salts.

The town is also known
for its production of
beautifully decorated
Karlovy Vary china and
brightly coloured Moser
Glass, and also for summer
concerts and other cultural

events, including an
annual international
film festival – one of the
world's oldest and most
prestigious –that takes
place in early June. As one
of Europe's leading film
events, it attracts a host
of international stars.

Outstanding among
the local historic monuments is the Baroque
parish church of Mary
Magdalene by Kilian Ignaz
Dientzenhofer. More
modern churches built for
foreign visitors include a
Russian church (in 1896)
and an Anglican one (in

1877). The 19th-century
Mill Colonnade (Mlýnská
kolonáda) is by Josef Zítek,
who was the architect of
the National Theatre.

Mariánské Lázně

🏠 170 km (105 miles) W of
Prague 🚆 From Hlavní
nádraží 🚌 From Florenc
ℹ️ Hlavní 47 (354 622 474)
🌐 marianskelazne.cz

This delightful spa town
lost in the forests of
West Bohemia once drew
royalty and celebrities
to its elegant parks and
spa houses. The area's
health-giving waters –
lázně means bath (or spa) –
have been known since
the 16th century, but
the spa was not founded
until the beginning of the
19th century. The mineral
waters are unusually high
in carbon dioxide and iron,
and used to treat all kinds
of health disorders;

→

River Teplá running through
central Karlovy Vary

Josef Vylet'al's cast-iron colonnade and the "singing fountain" in Mariánské Lázně

bathing in the mud baths is also popular.

Most of the spa buildings date from the latter half of the 19th century. The great cast-iron colonnade with frescoes by Josef Vylet'al is still an impressive sight. In front of it is a "singing fountain", its jets of water now controlled by computer. Churches were provided for visitors of all denominations, including an Evangelical church (1857), an Anglican church (1879) and the Russian Orthodox church of St Vladimír (1902). Visitors can learn about the history of the spa in the house called At the Golden Grape (U zlatého hroznu), where the German poet Johann Wolfgang von Goethe stayed in 1823. Musical visitors during the 19th century included the composers Weber, Wagner and Bruckner, while writers such as Ibsen, Gogol, Mark Twain and Rudyard Kipling also found its treatments beneficial. King Edward VII came here too, and in 1905 he agreed to open the golf course (Bohemia's first), despite hating the game.

SHOP

Moser Factory Shop

After visiting the Moser factory to see the glass blowers at work, stop by the factory shop to pick up a souvenir. Be prepared to part with a lot of money to acquire any of the creations.

🏠 Kpt. Jaroše 46/18, Karlovy Vary

🌐 moser.cz

Jan Becher Museum Shop

Becherovka is a herb-infused alcoholic liqueur made in the spa town of Karlovy Vary – the best place to buy a bottle is from the manufacturer's museum shop.

🏠 T.G. Masaryka 57, Karlovy Vary

🌐 becherovka.com

KV Suvenýry

This small shop within the elaborate, gently curving colonnade in Mariánské Lázně's spa zone sells a wide selection of good-quality souvenirs originating from across the entire country.

🏠 Main Colonnade, Mariánské Lázně

BEFORE YOU GO

Forward planning is essential to any successful trip. Be prepared for all eventualities by considering the following points before you travel.

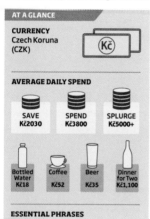

CURRENCY
Czech Koruna
(CZK)

AVERAGE DAILY SPEND

SAVE	SPEND	SPLURGE
Kč2030	Kč3800	Kč5000+

Bottled Water	Coffee	Beer	Dinner for Two
Kč18	Kč52	Kč35	Kč1,100

ESSENTIAL PHRASES

Hello	Dobrý den
Goodbye	Na shledanou
Please	Prosím
Thank you	Děkuji vám
Do you speak English?	Mluvíte anglicky?
I don't understand	Nerozumím

ELECTRICITY SUPPLY
Power sockets are type E, fitting two-pronged plugs. Standard voltage is 230 volts.

Passports and Visas

For a stay of up to three months for the purpose of tourism, EU nationals and citizens of the US, Canada, Australia and New Zealand do not need a visa. For visa information specific to your home country, consult your nearest Czech embassy or check online.
The Ministry of Foreign Affairs of the Czech Republic
W mzv.cz

Travel Safety Advice

Visitors can get up-to-date travel safety information from the **UK Foreign and Commonwealth Office**, the **US State Department**, and the **Australian Department of Foreign Affairs and Trade**.
AUS
W smartraveller.gov.au
UK
W gov.uk/foreign-travel-advice
US
W travel.state.gov

Customs Information

An individual is permitted to carry the following within the EU for personal use:
Tobacco products 800 cigarettes, 400 cigarillos, 200 cigars or 1 kg of smoking tobacco.
Alcohol 10 litres of alcoholic beverages above 22% strength, 20 litres of alcoholic beverages below 22% strength, 90 litres of wine (60 litres of which can be sparkling wine) and 110 litres of beer.
Cash If entering or leaving the EU with €10,000 or more in cash (or the equivalent in other currencies) it must be declared to the customs authorities.

If travelling outside the EU, limits vary so check restrictions before departing.

Insurance

It is wise to take out insurance that covers theft, loss, medical problems, cancellation and delays. EU citizens are eligible for free emergency medical care in the Czech Republic provided they have a valid **EHIC** (European Health Insurance Card).

Visitors from outside the EU must arrange their own private medical insurance.
EHIC
W gov.uk/european-health-insurance-card

Vaccinations

No inoculations are needed for travellers visiting the Czech Republic.

Money

Most establishments accept major credit, debit and prepaid currency cards. Contactless payments are becoming increasingly common, but it's always a good idea to carry some cash for smaller items and local markets.

Booking Accommodation

Prague offers a huge variety of accommodation, comprising luxury five-star hotels, family-run B&Bs and budget hostels.

Prices are often inflated during peak season (early and late summer, Easter and Christmas holidays), so it's worth booking well in advance. **Prague City Tourism** provides a list of accommodation to suit all needs.

Travellers with Specific Needs

Airport assistance is available for free but must be booked in advance through your airline or travel agency. Narrow streets and uneven paving make Prague difficult for wheelchair users. However, services are improving. Most public buildings are now fitted with entry ramps.

Most of the trams and buses have low access, and most of the metro stations are fitted with lifts. Timetables at tram stops indicate which services are wheelchair-accessible. Visit the **Prague Public Transport Company** website to plan your journey using wheelchair-accessible metro stations, trams and buses.

Accessible Prague can arrange transport from the airport to the city centre for wheelchair users and they offer tours tailored to visitors' needs. The **Prague Organisation of Wheelchair Users** has a range of resources available, including maps and guides in Braille.
Accessible Prague
W accessibleprague.com
Prague Organisation of Wheelchair Users
W presbariery.cz
Prague Public Transport Company
W dpp.cz/en/barrier-free-travel

Language

The Slavic language of Czech is the official language of the Czech Republic. English replaced Russian as the second language of choice after the Velvet Revolution (1989). Those working in the tourist industry usually have a good level of English, French, Russian and often German too, but it's appreciated if you know a few phrases in the local language.

Closures

Mondays Some museums and attractions are closed for the day.
Weekends Some shops close early on Saturdays and for the day on Sundays. Public transport runs a reduced service.
Public holidays Schools, banks and most public services are closed; shops, some museums and attractions close early or for the day.

GETTING AROUND

Whether exploring Prague's historic centre by foot or public transport, here you'll find all you need to know to navigate the city like a pro.

AT A GLANCE

PUBLIC TRANSPORT COSTS
Tickets are valid on all forms of public transport in Prague.

SHORT TRIP

Kč24

30 mins including transfers

SINGLE

Kč32

90 mins including transfers

DAY TICKET

Kč110

Unlimited travel

SPEED LIMIT

MOTORWAY	EXPRESSWAYS
130 km/h (81 mph)	**110** km/h (68 mph)

NATIONAL ROADS	URBAN AREAS
90 km/h (56 mph)	**50** km/h (31 mph)

Arriving by Air

More than 60 international airlines fly to Prague's Václav Havel Airport, situated 15 km (9 miles) northwest of the city centre in Ruzyně. The airport has three terminals. Terminal 1 is used for intercontinental flights to the UK, North America, the Middle East, Africa and Asia. All domestic flights and flights to destinations within the EU and other Schengen countries are served by Terminal 2. These two terminals are connected and are only a short walk apart. Terminal 3, also known as the South Terminal, is further away and used only for general aviation and private planes. Getting to and from Prague airport is easy, relatively fast and economical. Allow at least 60 minutes to reach the airport by road from the city centre at rush hour, though on a good day, it could take as little as 30 minutes. Travelling by a combination of the metro and standard bus takes about 45 minutes depending on connections. There is a shared shuttle bus run by **Prague Airport Shuttles** that goes to the city centre every 15 minutes for Kč290 per person. You can also request to be dropped off at your hotel or accommodation.
Prague Airport Shuttles
ⓦ prague-airport-shuttle.cz

Train Travel

International Train Travel
Regular high-speed international trains connect Prague's Hlavní nádraží and Nádraží Holešovice stations to other major cities across Europe. Reservations for these services are essential as seats book up quickly, particularly in the busy summer months. You can buy tickets and passes for multiple international journeys from **Eurail** or **Interrail**, however you may still need to pay an additional reservation fee depending on what

rail service you travel with. Always check that your pass is valid on the service on which you wish to travel before boarding. Students and those under the age of 26 can benefit from discounted rail travel. For more information on discounted rail travel both in and to the Czech Republic, visit the Interrail or Eurail website.

Eurail W eurail.com
Interrail W interrail.eu

Domestic Train Travel

The railways in the Czech Republic are run by České Dráhy (**ČD**). The biggest and busiest railway station in Prague is Hlavní nádraží, which is only a 5-minute walk from Wenceslas Square. After a thorough renovation, the Art Nouveau station now features a gleaming interior with shops, restaurants, a pub and even a jeweller's. The lower ground floor has an inexpensive leftluggage facility and the central ticket office (open 3:20am–00:30am). There is also a ČD Travel office, where all international rail tickets are available from multilingual station staff and ticket machines. There are several types of train services operating in Prague and throughout the Czech Republic, including the *rychlík* (express) trains; the *osobní* (passenger) trains which form a local service and stop at all stations; and the express, for longer distances. Tickets can be bought in advance. If you want to buy a ticket just before your train leaves, be aware that queues at ticket booths can be long. On the timetable, an "R" in a box by a train number means you must have a seat reserved on that train. An "R" without a box means a reservation is recommended. If you are caught in the wrong carriage, you have to pay an on-the-spot fine.

ČD W cd.cz

Public Transport

Prague's bus, tram and metro services are provided by the Prague Public Transport Company (**DPP**). The best way of getting around central Prague by public transport is by tram or metro. Prague's rush hours are between 6am and 9am and 3pm and 5pm, Monday to Friday. However, more trains, trams and buses run at these times, so crowding is not usually a problem. Some bus routes to the suburbs only run during peak hours. It is worth noting that the city centre is compact, and so most of the major sights are within walking distance of one another.

DPP W dpp.cz

Tickets

Prague has a fully integrated public transport system. As such, tickets are conveniently valid on all forms of public transport in the city, including bus, tram, metro, rail and boat services, and even the funicular railway that runs from Újezd to the top of Petřín Hill. Tickets are available from machines at metro stations, main tram stops and at most news stands (*tabák*) which can be found at various locations throughout the city. Buy tickets before you travel and validate them in the machines provided. Periodic checks are carried out by plain-clothes ticket inspectors who will levy a large on-the-spot fine if you are caught without a valid ticket. Children under 6 travel free and tickets for children aged 6–15 are half price. Individual ticket prices add up; longer-term tickets are good value if you are planning on exploring the city thoroughly. Network tickets offer unlimited travel for a set number of days. Tickets are available for one day (Kč110) and three days (Kč310).

Buses

Visitors are likely to use a bus only to travel to and from the airport, or to sights further out of town such as the zoo. Three bus lines operate in Malá Strana Old Town and New Town and are operated by small vehicles. Night buses (routes 901–915) operate from midnight to 4:30am. Usual fares apply. Bus timetables are located at every stop. Daytime buses run 5am–midnight every 6–30 minutes. Night buses run midnight–4:30am every 20–60 minutes. Tickets bought on board are more expensive and can be paid for in cash only. Validate your pre-bought tickets in the machine located at each door.

Long-Distance Bus Travel

Long-distance bus or coach travel can be a cheap option for those visiting Prague. Some Czech towns, such as Karlovy Vary, Hradec Králové, Český Krumlov and Terezin, are much easier to reach by coach than train. The city's main bus terminal is Florenc, on the north-eastern edge of the New Town. **Eurolines** offer a variety of routes to Prague from other European cities. **Flixbus** and **RegioJet** also offer several domestic routes.

Eurolines W eurolines.eu; **Flixbus** W flixbus.com; **RegioJet** W regiojet.com

Trams

The city's comprehensive tram network covers a large area, including the city centre. Maps and timetables at tram stops help you locate your destination and route. On the timetable, the stop you are at will be underlined and stops below the line will indicate where the tram is heading. The direction of travel is given by the terminus station. Routes 9, 14, 17 and 22 are the most useful for getting around the centre of Prague. They pass many of the major sights on both sides of the Vltava, and are a cheap and pleasant way of sightseeing. Night trams (routes 91–99) run every 30 minutes and are marked by white numbers on a dark background at the stop. Trams run 4:30am–12:30am daily every 4–20 minutes. Tram tickets are also valid for travel on the metro and buses, but they must be bought before travel. Validate your ticket in the yellow machines on board.

Metro

The metro is the fastest way to get around the city. Prague's underground system comprises three lines (A, B and C) operating from 5am until midnight every 1–4 minutes at peak times during weekdays (6–9am and 3–5pm daily), and every 4–10 minutes during off-peak times. Line A (green) is the most useful for tourists, covering all the main areas of the city centre – Prague Castle, Malá Strana, the Old Town and the New Town – including the main shopping area around Wenceslas Square. Stations are signposted in both English and Czech.

Taxis

All taxis in Prague are privately owned, and there are many unscrupulous drivers who are out to charge as much as they can get away with. If you think you have been scammed by a taxi driver, take their name and number so you can report them to the police. Look for Fair Place taxi ranks marked with a yellow "taxi" sign and an orange "thumbs up" icon. Taxis that stop here will guarantee the maximum charges of Kč40 boarding fee, Kč28 per km travel and Kč6 per minute waiting. After the journey, the driver is obliged to print an official receipt. Taxi companies that are safe to hail on the street include **AAA Taxi** and **Profi Taxi**. However, the cheapest way to get a taxi is to phone or use the company's mobile app. Unless your Czech pronunciation is very good, it is useful to have your destination written down in Czech.

AAA Taxi W aaataxi.cz
Profi Taxi W profitaxi.cz

Driving

Driving in Prague is not recommended. The city's complex web of one-way streets, lack of parking and pedestrianized areas make driving very difficult.

Driving to Prague

The Czech Republic is easily reached by car from most countries in eastern, central and southern Europe via E-roads, the International European Road Network. Prague is connected to every major border crossing by motorways (D roads) and expressways (R roads). To drive on the motorway you will need to display a special highway toll sticker available at the border, petrol stations and post offices.

Car Rental

To rent a car in the Czech Republic, you must be at least 21 years old and have held a valid licence for at least one year. Drivers under the age of 26 may incur a young driver surcharge. EU driving licences issued by any of the EU member states are valid throughout the European Union. If visiting from outside the EU, you may need to apply for an International Driving Permit (IDP). Check with your local automobile association before you travel.

Driving in Prague

Beware of cyclists and trams in the city. Trams take precedence; take care when turning; and allow cyclists priority. Vehicles must be parked on the right hand side of the road only, with the exception of one-way streets. Parking spaces in the centre are scarce, and the penalties for illegal parking are harsh. **Parkuj v klidu** provide detailed information regarding parking. Meter parking from 8am to 8pm costs a maximum Kč80 per hour. Orange zones allow parking for two hours and violet zones for a maximum of 24; blue zones are reserved for residents. To use the meter, insert coins for the amount of time you need. The inspection is done automatically by the monitoring system based on the registration mark (license plate) of the vehicle. Unfortunately, car theft is rife. Try to park in an official – preferably underground – car park or at one of the guarded car parks (look for the "P+R" symbol) at the edge of the city and use public transport to travel in. If a car accident occurs, the vehicle cannot be moved until there has been a police inspection. In case of emergency, you can call the road traffic assistance, Autoklub Bohemia Assistance (**ÚAMK**), on the phone number 1240.
Parkuj v klidu W parkujvklidu.cz
ÚAMK W uamk.cz

Rules of the Road

Always drive on the right. Unless otherwise signposted, vehicles coming from the right have right of way. At all times, drivers must carry a valid driver's licence, registration and insurance documents. Both driver and front- and back-seat passengers must wear seat belts. Small kids must travel in the back seat. The use of a mobile phone while driving is strictly prohibited, with the exception of a hands-free system. Speed limits and a zero tolerance drink-driving policy are strictly enforced in Prague.

Cycling

Prague is generally a bike-friendly city, with many designated cycle lanes.

Bicycle Hire

Bicycles can be rented hourly or by the day. Deposits are usually paid upfront and refunded on return. You may have to leave a valid passport or driver's licence for the duration of the rental. **Praha Bike** offers private rentals and tours. Public bicycle schemes such as **Rekola**, which is operated through an app, are also available. As part of the **Prague–Vienna Greenways Project**, well-maintained bike paths line both sides of the Vltava, and there are a number of biking trails linking Prague and Vienna. Details of other bike tours and excursions are available from Prague City Tourism.
Prague–Vienna Greenways Project
W pragueviennagreenways.org; **Praha Bike**
W prahabike.cz; **Rekola W** rekola.cz

Bicycle Safety

Ride on the right. If in doubt, dismount; if you do so, switch to the pedestrian section of the crossing. Beware of tram tracks; cross them at an angle to avoid getting stuck. For your own safety, do not walk with your bike in a bike lane or cycle on pavements, on the left side of the road, in pedestrian zones, or in the dark without lights. Wearing a helmet is recommended.

Prague by Boat

Regular transport tickets are also valid on the public boat service (lines P1–6). Boat tours along the Vltava river allow for fabulous views of Prague's major sights. Most run during the summer months. Check out **Prague Boats** or **Evropská Vodní Doprava**.
Prague Boats W prague-boats.cz;
Evropská Vodní Doprava W evd.cz

PRACTICAL INFORMATION

A little local know-how goes a long way in Prague. Here you will find all the essential advice and information you will need during your stay.

EMERGENCY NUMBERS

GENERAL EMERGENCY	POLICE
112	**158**

AMBULANCE	FIRE SERVICE
155	**150**

TIME ZONE
CET/CEST
Central European Summer Time (CEST) runs end Mar–end Oct.

TAP WATER
Tap water in Prague is safe to drink.

TIPPING

Waiter	10%
Hotel Porter	Kč40 per bag
Housekeeping	Kč20 per day
Concierge	Kč20–40
Taxi Driver	Not expected

Personal Security

Pickpockets work crowds and busy areas. Use your common sense and be alert to your surroundings. Never leave anything of value in your car as break-ins are rife. If you have anything stolen, report the crime as soon as possible to the nearest police station, and bring ID with you. Get a copy of the crime report in order to claim on your insurance. If you have your passport stolen, or if you are involved in a serious crime or accident, contact your embassy as soon as possible.

Health

For minor ailments and prescriptions go to a pharmacy (lékárna). Details of the nearest 24-hour service are usually displayed in pharmacy windows. EU citizens carrying a valid **EHIC** card are eligible for free emergency medical care in the Czech Republic. If travelling from outside the EU, payment of hospital bills and other medical expenses is the patient's responsibility. As such it is important to arrange comprehensive medical insurance before your departure. You may have to pay upfront for medical treatment and reclaim on your insurance later.

Smoking, Alcohol and Drugs

Prague has a strict smoking ban in all public spaces including public buildings, bars, cafés, shops, restaurants and hotels. The possession of narcotics is prohibited. Possession of illegal substances could result in prosecution and a prison sentence. There is no blanket ban on the consumption of alcohol on the streets; however, drinking alcohol on the bus or train and in metro stations, parks, playgrounds and near schools is banned and may incur a fine.

Many Old Town streets have banned walking around with an open bottle or can. The Czech Republic enforces a strict zero tolerance policy on drink-driving. This also applies to cyclists.

ID

It is compulsory for visitors to carry a form of ID at all times, or failing that, a photocopy of your passport.

Local Customs

The Czechs are fiercely proud of their language and its difficult pronunciation, often finding foreigners' attempts at speaking it amusing. Avoid overzealous tipping – this can cause embarrassment to waiting staff.

Visiting Churches and Cathedrals

Dress respectfully: cover your torso and upper arms; ensure shorts and skirts cover your knees.

Mobile Phones and Wi-Fi

Free Wi-Fi hotspots are widely available in Prague's city centre. Cafés and restaurants usually permit the use of their Wi-Fi on the condition that you make a purchase.

Visitors travelling to Prague with EU tariffs can use their devices abroad without being affected by data roaming charges. Users will be charged the same rates for data, SMS and voice calls as they would pay at home.

Post

Stamps can be bought from post offices, newsagents and tobacconists (tabák).

Parcels and registered letters must be sent from a post office. There is no first- or second-class mail, but the majority of letters usually arrive at their destination within a few days.

Taxes and Refunds

VAT in the Czech Republic is usually around 20% for most items. Non-EU residents are entitled to a tax refund on single purchases exceeding Kč2000, subject to certain conditions. This does not include tobacco or alcohol. When you make a purchase, ask the sales assistant for a tax-free cheque. When leaving the country, present this form, along with the goods receipt and your ID at customs.

Discount Cards

There are a number of passes or discount cards available to tourists visiting the city. Most offer free or discounted access to Prague's top sights, including exhibitions, museums and tours. Some even cover transport costs.

The cards are not free, so consider carefully how many of the offers you are likely to take advantage of before purchasing to ensure you get a good deal.

Prague City Card Entry to 50 attractions and discounted entry to 50 more, free travel on public transport and airport transfers, and discounted tours, cruises and concerts for two (Kč1550), three (Kč1810) or four (Kč2080) days. Available from participating tourist offices.

The Prague City Pass Free or discounted entry to Prague's most popular tours and attractions. The card costs Kč1390 and is valid for 30 days from first use. Available online and from participating tourist offices.

The Prague Welcome Card Entry to over 50 attractions, discounts on tours, events and more, plus free travel on public transport. The card costs Kč1050 and is valid for 3 days from first use. Available online and from participating tourist offices.

Prague City Card Ⓦ praguecard.com
Prague City Pass Ⓦ praguecitypass.com
Prague Welcome Card Ⓦ praguewelcome
card.com

INDEX

ACKNOWLEDGMENTS

Dorling Kindersley would like to extend special thanks to the following people for their contribution: Anamika Bhandari, Syed Mohammad Farhan, Shanker Prasad, Rohit Rojal.

The publisher would like to thank the following for their kind permission to reproduce their photographs:

Key: a-above; b-below/bottom; c-centre; f-far; l-left; r-right; t-top

123RF.com: Goran Bogicevic 90-11c; Svetlana Day 12-3b; emicristea 22br, 47c.

4Corners: Luigi Vaccarella 17b.

Alamy Stock Photo: a-plus image bank 59tr; Arazu 57t, 57br; Austrian National Library / Interfoto 81tr; Sergio Azenha 78b; Oliver Benn 45tr; Petr Bonek 95cra; Alena Brozova 47cl; CTK / Fluger Rene 86b; Lucie Debelkova 52-3tc; emka74 68br; Kirk Fisher 70b; Shaun Higson 37br; Nataliya

Hora 2t; kaprik 85tr; John Kellerman 55tl; Art Kowalsky 45cr; John McKenna 59br; B.O'Kane 15t, 89tr; PjrTravel 13tl; David Robertson 39tl; Jorge Royan 13cr; Slawek Staszczuk 18tl; tilialucida 45tl; Steve Tulley 83cl; Lucas Vallecillos 29bl; wanderluster 63cra.

Depositphotos Inc: anmbph 77crb; seregalsv 38b; vladvitek 101tr.

Dorling Kindersley: National Music Museum / Gary Ombler 72bl; Jiri Kopriva 44clb.

Dreamstime.com: Anton Aleksenko 16tl; Alonfridman 69tr; Lukas Blazek 66t; Daliu80 60-1t; Doethion 88b; Dziewul 55br; Sergey Dzyuba 14bl; Oliver Förstner 34b; Filip Fuxa 99tr; GoneWithTheWind 82-3b; Dmitry Ilyshev 64br; David Jancik 62cl; Jjfarq 39tc; Jorisvo 20b; Kaprik 6b, 91cl; Ktree 41crb; Laudibi 67bl;

Roman Milert 26b; Jaroslav Moravcik 27t, 30clb, 47tl; Luciano Mortula 3tl; Roman Plesky 21tr; Pp1 92clb; Radomír Režný 50b, 73tr; Richard Semik 75br, 94b; Anton Shevialiukhin 84br; Petr Švec 98-9b; Thecriss 83tc; Tomas1111 32t; Tuomaslehtinen 75tl; Richard Van Der Woude 46-7b; Yakub88 41bc.

Getty Images: Corbis / Rob Tilley 96t; LightRocket / Wolfgang Kaehler 36tr.

iStockphoto.com: alxpin 41br; DaLiu 4-5b; Andrey Danilovich 58-9b; Tatiana Dyuvbanova 95tl; E+ / Nikada 79tl; InnaFelker 11tl; Kirillm 61crb; letty17 100br; mpalis 93tl; Nikada 7br; PleskyRoman 25tl; PytyCzech 80bl; rapier 43tr; TomasSereda 56b; wrangel 10bc.

Robert Harding Picture Library: Karl Johaentges 49bl.

For further information see:
www.dkimages.com

PHRASE BOOK

IN EMERGENCY

Help!	Pomoc!	po-*mots*
Stop!	Zastavte!	za-*stav-te*
Call a doctor!	Zavolejte doktora!	za-*vo-ley-te* dok-*to-ra!*
Call an ambulance!	Zavolejte sanitku!	za-*vo-ley-te* sa-*nit-ku!*
Call the police!	Zavolejte policii!	za-*vo-ley-te* poli-*tsi-yi!*
Call the fire brigade!	Zavolejte hasiče	za-*vo-lay-te* ha-*si-che*
Where is the telephone?	Kde je telefón?	gde ye tele-*fohn?*
the nearest hospital?	nejbližší nemocnice?	ney-*blish-ee* ne-*mots-nyitse?*

COMMUNICATION ESSENTIALS

Yes/No	Ano/Ne	ano/ne
Please	Prosím	pro-*seem*
Thank you	Děkuji vám	dye-*ku-ji* vahm
Excuse me	Prosím vás	pro-*seem* vahs
Hello	Dobrý den	do-*bree* den
Goodbye	Na shledanou	na s-*hle-da-no*
Good evening	Dobrý večer	doh-*ree* vech-*er*
morning	ráno	rah-*no*
afternoon	odpoledne	od-*po-led-ne*
evening	večer	ve-*cher*
yesterday	včera	vche-*ra*
today	dnes	dnehs
tomorrow	zítra	zeet-*ra*
here	tady	ta-*di*
there	tam	tam
What?	Co?	tso?
When?	Kdy?	gdi?
Why?	Proč?	proch?
Where?	Kde?	gde?

USEFUL PHRASES

How are you?	Jak se máte?	yak-*se* mah-*te?*
Very well, thank you.	Velmi dobře děkuji.	vel-*mi* dob-*rzhe de kuyi*
Pleased to meet you.	Těší mě.	tyesh-*ee mye*

See you soon.	Uvidíme se brzy.	u-*vi-dyee-me-se-br-zi*
That's fine.	To je v pořádku.	to ye vpo-*rzhahdku*
Where is/ are...?	Kde jsou...?	gde ye/ yso...?
How long does it take to get to¨?	Jak dlouho to trvá se dostat do..?	yak dlo ho to tr-*va* se do-*stat do...?*
How do I get to...?	Jak se dostanu k..?	yak se do-*sta-nuk...?*
Do you speak English?	Mluvíte anglicky?	mlu -*vee-te* an -*glits-ki?*
I don't understand.	Nerozumím.	ne -*ro-zu-meem*
Could you speak more slowly?	Mohl(a)* byste mluvit trochu pomaleji?	mohl- *(a)* bis-*te* mlu-*vit* tro-*khu po-maley?*
Pardon?	Prosím?	pro-*seem?*
I'm lost.	Ztratil(a)* jsem se.	stra-*tyil (a)* y*sem se.*

USEFUL WORDS

big	velký	vel-*kee*
small	malý	mal-*ee*
hot	horký	hor-*kee*
cold	studený	stu-*den-ee*
good	dobrý	dob-*ree*
bad	špatný	shpat-*nee*
well	dobře	dob-*rzhe*
open	otevřeno	ot-*ev-rzhe-no*
closed	zavřeno	zav-*rzhe-no*
left	do leva	do le-*va*
right	do prava	do pra-*va*
straight on	rovně	rov-*nye*
near	blízko	blee-*sko*
far	daleko	da-*le-ko*
up	nahoru	na-*ho-ru*
down	dolů	do-*loo*
early	brzy	br-*zi*
late	pozdě	poz-*dye*
entrance	vchod	vkhod
exit	východ	vee-*khod*
toilets	toalety	toa-*leti*
free, unoccupied	volný	vol-*nee*
free, no charge	zdarma	zdar-*ma*